THE QUESTION ⊙. ...

For Claire

[signature]

12.09

THE QUESTION OF MORALE
Managing happiness and unhappiness in university life

David Watson

 Open University Press

Open University Press
McGraw-Hill Education
McGraw-Hill House
Shoppenhangers Road
Maidenhead
Berkshire
England
SL6 2QL

email: enquiries@openup.co.uk
world wide web: www.openup.co.uk

and Two Penn Plaza, New York, NY 10121–2289, USA

First published 2009
Copyright © David Watson 2009

All rights reserved. Except for the quotation of short passages for the purposes of criticism and review, no part of this publication may be reproduced, stored in a retrieval system, or transmitted, in any form or by any means, electronic, mechanical, photocopying, recording or otherwise, without the prior permission of the publisher or a licence from the Copyright Licensing Agency Limited. Details of such licences (for reprographic reproduction) may be obtained from the Copyright Licensing Agency Ltd of Saffron House, 6–10 Kirby Street, London, EC1N 8TS.

A catalogue record of this book is available from the British Library

ISBN–10: 0335235603 (pb) 033523559X (hb)
ISBN–13: 9780335235605 (pb) 9780335235599 (hb)

Library of Congress Cataloguing-in-Publication Data

Typeset by YHT Ltd, London
Printed in the UK by Bell and Bain Ltd., Glasgow

Mixed Sources
Product group from well-managed
forests and other controlled sources
www.fsc.org Cert no. TT-COC-002769
© 1996 Forest Stewardship Council

FSC

The *McGraw·Hill* Companies

In memoriam

Hazel Bines (1950–2009)
Ronald Dearing (1930–2009)

CONTENTS

LIST OF FIGURES

LIST OF TABLES

FOREWORD

David Watson is a historian of ideas. However, for the last 35 years he has also been a manager of various enterprises within UK higher education: a course leader, a dean, a governor, a polytechnic deputy director and director, and a university vice-chancellor, as well as a participant in a whole range of activities and obligations outside the academy. This book shows how these worlds combine: those of the academic, the manager, the academic manager, and the manager of academics, as well as the advocate of what higher education means to society, and how it could mean more.

It also juxtaposes scholarly references to relevant work in a variety of fields – history, sociology, anthropology, philosophy and literature – with some valuable testimony (especially in the frequent 'digressions') from the front line. Watson's take is personal, sometimes idiosyncratic. There is an extraordinary range of references, representing his 'hinterland': from Ian Fleming and Mike Brearley, through Charles Ives to Martin Heidegger. But there is also thoughtful and analytical depth.

The effect is to offer a sensitive and, I think, substantially convincing account of our present situation. The picture of a university where collective understanding, trust and commitment is sufficient to maintain strategic direction, local innovation and satisfactory levels of self-care is an attractive one. Positive university morale is elusive, but worth the struggle to establish and then to maintain. There are some helpful hints here on how to achieve these elusive goals, but nothing like a rigid formula. Above all, Watson shows the power and the value of the effort.

Professor Sir Peter Scott
Vice-chancellor, University of Kingston
President, Association of University Administrators (AUA)
Chair, Universities Association for Lifelong
Learning (UALL)

ABBREVIATIONS

AAUP	American Association of University Professors
AB	academic board
ACE	American Council on Education
ACT	adult and continuing education
ASHE	Annual Survey of Hours and Earnings
ASN	additional student numbers
ASS	Association of Seaside Universities
AUA	Association of University Administrators
AUT	Association of University Teachers
BBC	British Broadcasting Corporation
CAP	changing nature of the academic profession
CBI	Confederation of British Industry
CBT	cognitive behavioural therapy
CEDR	Centre for Effective Dispute Resolution
CEO	chief executive officer
CHE	*Chronicle of Higher Education*
CHEMS	Commonwealth Higher Education Management Services
CIHE	Council of Industry and Higher Education
CMC	Civil Mediation Council
CMI	Chartered Management Institute
CNAA	Council for National Academic Awards
CPD	continuous professional development
CUC	Committee of University Chairmen
DfES	Department for Education and Skills
DipHE	Diploma of Higher Education
DIUS	Department for Innovation, Universities and Science
DVC	deputy vice-chancellor

ECHR	European Convention on Human Rights
ELQ	equivalent or lower qualifications
ESA	Executive Search Agency
ESF	European Science Foundation
ESRC	Economic and Social Research Council
ET	employment tribunal
EU	European Union
Fd	foundation degree
FE	further education
FOI	Freedom of Information Act
FSSG	Financial Sustainability Strategy Group
GB	governing body
GNH	gross national happiness
GOC	General Osteopathic Council
GOS	Government Office of Science
HBS	Harvard Business School
HE	higher education
HEA	Higher Education Academy
HEFCE	Higher Education Funding Council for England
HEI	higher education institution
HEM	higher education management
HEPI	Higher Education Policy Institute
HESA	Higher Education Statistics Agency
HMI	Her Majesty's Inspectorate
HMSO	Her Majesty's Stationery Office
HND	Higher National Diploma
HR	human resources
ICT	information and communications technology
IFLL	Inquiry into the Future for Lifelong Learning
IOD	Institute of Directors
IoE	Institute of Education, University of London
ISI	Intercollegiate Studies Institute
KCL	King's College, London
LERU	League of European Research Universities
LFHE	Leadership Foundation for Higher Education
LSN	Learning and Skills Network
LT	leadership team
MBA	Master of Business Administration
MP	Member of Parliament
NATFHE	National Association of Teachers in Further and Higher Education
NCIHE	National Commission of Inquiry into Higher Education (Dearing Report)
NEF	New Economics Foundation

NSS	National Student Survey
NUS	National Union of Students
OFFA	Office for Fair Access
OfSTED	Office for Standards in Education
OIA	Office of the Independent Adjudicator
OxCHEPS	Oxford Centre for Higher Education Policy Studies
PRP	Penn Resilience Program (Seligman)
PRP	permission/reconstruction/perspective (Ben-Shahar)
PRP	performance-related pay
PSB	professional and statutory bodies
PVC	pro-vice-chancellor
QAA	Quality Assurance Agency for Higher Education
R&D	research and development
RAE	research assessment exercise
RCUK	Research Councils UK
SEAL	social and emotional aspects of learning
SEEDA	South East England Development Agency
SL	senior lecturer
SOMUL	social and organizational mediation of university learning
SRHE	Society for Research into Higher Education
SSR	student:staff ratio
STEM	science, technology, engineering and mathematics (sometimes medicine)
SUNY	State University of New York
TDAP	taught degree-awarding powers
THE	Times Higher Education
THES	*Times Higher Education Supplement*
TLRP	Teaching and Learning Research Programme
UALL	Universities Association for Lifelong Learning
UCEA	Universities and Colleges Employers' Association
UCL	University College London
UCU	Universities and Colleges Union
UHI	University of the Highlands and Islands Millennium Institute
UKRIO	UK Research Integrity Research Office
UN	United Nations
UNICEF	United Nations Children's Fund
USP	unique selling point
UUK	Universities UK
VC	vice-chancellor

1

INTRODUCTION: WHY MORALE?

The research questions I attempt to answer in this book include the following. Why is so much discourse about contemporary higher education structured around (real and imagined) unhappiness? How does this connect with the realities of life within (and just outside) the institutions? Does it matter, and, if so, what should we be doing about it?

There is a comforting tale that vice-chancellors (VCs) of UK higher education institutions (HEIs) like to tell each other. 'Go around your university or college,' they say, 'and ask the first 10 people who you meet how their morale is. The response will always be "rock bottom". Then ask them what they are working on. The responses will be full of life, of optimism and of enthusiasm for the task in hand.' The moral of the story is that the two sets of responses don't compute; that the first is somehow unthinking and ideological, and the second unguarded and sincere.

In a broader setting, Adrian Furnham captures this asymmetry accurately in discussing 'the M-word' in his wonderful *Management and Myths*:

Morale is both the property of individuals and groups. Ask people about their personal morale, that of their (smallish) work group, their department and that of the organisation as a whole and you see a clear pattern. Climate surveys invariably show that most people believe that they have good morale, as do their personal work friends and colleagues, but they are pretty unsure about the department. And they certainly believe that overall company morale is low and probably steadily declining.

(Furnham 2004: 107)

This book will report on several surveys. A recent one at my own institution (the Institute of Education, University of London [IoE]) sought to discover feelings about 'an inclusive environment', where 'all staff are treated with dignity and respect'. The results were pure Furnham:

Using a survey distributed to all staff (35.5% response rate) the research provides a picture of an environment where feelings of trust, respect and mutual support are felt strongly at team level (76% agreement), but decline at Faculty/ Support Department level to 56% and fall to a disturbing 31% at [Institute] level.

(Schneider and Walmsley 2008: 3)

Nor is this just a UK phenomenon. The first reports from the Australian application of an international project on the 'Changing Nature of the Academic Profession' (CAP), repeat these results almost word for word. Leo Goedegebuure and his colleagues have created through CAP two 'modal' Australian academics: Colin and Cheryl (both born in 1960 and graduating in 1985):

They feel they have a fair bit of influence over what goes on at the departmental level, a little at the school level, but not very much at the institutional level. Most illustrative in this respect are the scores on the 'not at all influential' category: 22% at the department level, 48% at the school level and 57% at the institutional level.

(Goedegebuure *et al.* 2008: 17)

Colin and Cheryl would also validate the VC's story (above):

Overall, Colin and Cheryl would appear to be rather satisfied with their academic life. They score very high (14%) to high (55%) on the direct satisfaction question, whilst only 13% indicate low or very low (7%) satisfaction. This picture is confirmed by fairly strong disagreement with the statement 'If I had to do it over again, I would not become an academic' (mean 3.60, sd 1.296 on a scale of 1–5 with 1 = strongly agree), and an almost neutral score on the statement that the current job is a source of considerable personal strain (mean 2.65, sd 1.258).

These survey results are the more remarkable when we take into account the fact that many Australian academics are of the opinion that working conditions in higher education have deteriorated. Almost two-thirds of respondents believe that this is the case, with a very even distribution between those who think it has deteriorated and those who think that this has been very much the case. Only some 9% feel that working conditions have improved since the start of their career.

(Goedegebuure *et al.* 2008: 13)

The thesis of this book is that such contradictory answers may well compute more effectively than is acknowledged: that the culture of higher education (HE) and the mesh of psychological contracts, or 'deals,' that it involves make much of the current discourse about happiness and unhappiness in contemporary life look simplistic and banal. 'Academic' discourse is especially prone to paradox and plain inconsistency. Here are a few such statements – only mildly edited in the interests of clarity – from a strategic discussion with the senior academic leaders of what has to be, in anybody's league tables, one of the world's 'top' universities:

- We don't have enough money to do our jobs properly, but we are really good at them.
- We are severely oppressed, but we are also happy in our work.
- The government should support higher education better, and it should do this by giving us (our university) more than them (that other university).
- We can't give students what they really need, but it is our duty to attract the very best to come to study with us.
- In attracting these highly qualified students, what counts is the quality of our research, not of our teaching.
- The league tables are terrible, but we must climb them, and the higher we climb the less publicly we shall criticize them.

I felt, as a result of this discussion, the force of a very profound moral undertow. By saying that morale is anything other than rock bottom, the participants felt that they would be (a) reducing pressure on those 'others' responsible for it (especially 'managers' and 'funders') and (b) letting the side down. Nuance or qualification, or any sense of direction other than down, was just not possible.

Sometimes, of course, the schizophrenia can be more than tactical. It can even be playful or ironic. One participant in the institutional 'story-telling' exercise described in Chapter 6 gave two answers to the challenge of describing his/her university in 50 words or less.

A very large, post-1992 institution co-located with other providers in an inner-city area. Through acquisition and merger it now has seven geographically dispersed faculties currently being restructured onto three sites. There are pockets of research excellence but its main strengths lie in co-construction and delivery of employer-facing professional courses.

OR

A former poly that wants to be a Russell Group ivory tower, but has to rely on teaching and enterprise. Undergoing a major change agenda, a deeply unhappy place with low staff morale and a bullying management style where the left hand often doesn't know what the right is doing.

Which of these institutions does the witness live inside and work for? Perhaps it is both of them. If it is, how often does the scenery change: weekly, daily or hourly?

In particular, as I hope to demonstrate, the much-vaunted 'science of happiness' may not have much to say to us. There is also a potential linguistic link between the Manichean discourse about morale and our wider culture's approach to happiness. Both normally deal in extremes, and much more rarely in graduations. Professor Desmond Bates, David Lodge's latest (and perhaps most confessional) alter ego, as he struggles with the relentless onset of deafness, muses about the appearance in English of qualifiers or lexical collocates:

> It surprised me that the most common adverbs qualifying *happy* in the corpus were *entirely* and *perfectly*, rather than, say, 'fairly' or 'reasonably'. Are we ever entirely, perfectly happy? If so, it's not for very long. [Meanwhile] *entirely happy* is frequently preceded by *not* or some other negative word like *never*. But *perfectly* is usually unqualified.
>
> (Lodge 2008: 233)

In his masterly survey, *The Pursuit of Happiness*, Darrin McMahon quotes Primo Levi to similar effect. Even in the most extreme of personal circumstances, the temptation to look for the ideal and its antithesis is hard to break; but, says Levi, it is essential if we are to cling on to our humanity:

> Sooner or later in life everyone discovers that perfect happiness is unrealizable, but there are few who pause to consider the antithesis: that perfect unhappiness is equally unattainable. The obstacles preventing the realization of both these extreme states

are of the same nature: they derive from our human condition,
which is opposed to everything infinite.

(Levi in McMahon 2006: 457)

This does not, of course, prevent the discussion of happiness and
unhappiness in hyperbolic terms, not least in universities. The juxtaposition of these issues with the question of *morale* is deliberate. As
a term, 'morale' began as a synonym for morality, ethical principles
and practice, including their teaching. During the early nineteenth
century it shifted to refer more to conduct and behaviour, especially
(says the *Oxford English Dictionary*) with application to 'a body of
troops'. Today, Morale (deliberately capitalized) – in the sense of
esprit de corps – is a particular expression of collective happiness or
unhappiness. Although it has been traditionally connected with
military groups and nations at war, it is frequently invoked in peculiar communities like universities, which do see themselves as in
some senses special and apart, as well as frequently under siege.

Morale is essentially an 'inside out' issue: us against the world. This
book is also about various 'outside in' perspectives: how the world
sees us. Often this is through a frame of 'moral panic'. HE moral
panics come in various packets.

There is a set that is about behaviour. These include student excesses like drinking, hazing and initiation rites, cheating, and of-
fences against the neighbourhood (sometimes summed up as
'studentification'). Staff can be in the frame too, with accusations of
indifference, of bullying, or of misuse of academic freedom. Both
students and staff can be accused of failing to 'understand the real
world', especially of employment, but also of lack of manners and
civic responsibility.

Another set is about outcomes, especially standards. The part of
cheating that is 'plagiarism' enters here, as well as any variety of
academic dishonesty. Structurally the system can be accused of failure, as degrees become apparently easier (especially when measured
by the increase in frequency of 'good honours degrees') or the curriculum loses its bearings (as in so-called 'Mickey Mouse degrees').
The journalistic term for both of these is 'dumbing down'. Meanwhile, the inaccessibility of Oxbridge (and a wider – rather vague –
category of 'top universities') to non-standard students is lamented
at the same time as the prospect of what admitting them would do to
entry qualifications (and the interests of those who have expensively
purchased the positional advantage associated with high grades).

Then there are the panics about what is happening in the world
outside: the apparent ineluctable forces against which it is fashionable to rail, most of which are accompanied by their reciprocals. HE

is seen as a hotbed of 'commodification', 'instrumentality' and 'utilitarianism', at the same time as its unworldliness is lamented. There is anxiety about student 'consumers' exercising their right to demand better service, supported by intrusive 'helicopter parents', at the same time as they are urged to have a sense of value for money and to calculate the lifetime earnings effects of their degrees against the fees they have to pay. Students are criticized for working for money while studying (and thereby potentially damaging their academic prospects), while being urged to be independent and self-reliant. Meanwhile, in another part of the forest there are panics about either student apathy (when compared with the revolutionary utopianism of their predecessors), or fundamentalist zeal and the function of HEIs in incubating 'terrorist cells' and the like. In these circumstances, HE leaders and managers wonder if they can ever win the battle for media hearts and minds.

Most of these categories dissolve into a fourth (perhaps the most unempirical of all): the 'world we have lost'. Nostalgia rules. The media says that it wants modern, skills-rich, accessible HE but in fact its image of HE is derived from *Brideshead Revisited*. And rather than trying to lead them to a new place, the politicians both fuel and follow this particular crowd.

At the time of writing, global HE is also assessing how it will fare in the so-called 'credit crunch' (the collapse of both international and domestic financial systems in the wake of rampant personal, corporate and public debt). In these circumstances, HE systems are under the same pressures as any large complex organization. They are already suffering from a fall in the value of endowments, from trading difficulties, from uncertainties about off-balance sheet financial commitments, from currency fluctuations and the like.

However, because of their peculiar situation, there are a number of areas of distinctive uncertainty about what will happen to them and how much freedom they will have to manage their own destinies. The experience is also likely to be different in the developed and the developing world, with the usual prospect of the developing world's more modest HE infrastructures acting as a kind of header tank for developed systems.

Writing in the *New York Review of Books* Paul Krugman, the scourge of Bushian neo-liberal economics and diplomacy, comes up with a number of unsurprising conclusions. The first should be clear. It is about the global interdependence of both the problem and the solution: 'Everyone should be doing more or less the same thing; we're all in this together'. The second is about the traditional nature of the most strongly indicated response: 'The answer, almost surely is good old Keynesian fiscal stimulus.' The third is about the necessary

reassertion of public responsibility. For example, in terms of regulation, 'the basic principle should be clear: anything that has to be
rescued during a financial crisis, because it plays an essential role in
the financial mechanism, should be regulated when there *isn't* a
crisis'. He concludes with a reminder of Keynes' basic principle,
about 'the power of ideas': 'the true scarcity in Keynes' world – and
ours – was therefore not of resources, or even of virtue, but of understanding' (Krugman 2008). Universities have to be part of any
restoration of understanding.

Many of these uncertainties can be presented – in the spirit of
Robert Frost (1920) – as a fork in the road: 'Two roads diverged in a
wood':

> Two roads diverged in a wood, and I—
> I took the one less travelled by,
> And that has made all the difference.

Here are ten examples of 'two roads in a wood' as they might affect
HE:

- The first is about the student market. Will it become more or less
  instrumental in choice of courses and subjects? Will the requirements of the job market loom larger or less so? Will students want
  to accelerate or (as has happened in the past) delay their entry or
  re-entry into the job market? Will those who are able to choose
  want to travel or stay close to home?
- The second is about public investment. If there is a revival of
  Keynesian pump-priming (as Krugman suggests) in developed
  economies, will universities benefit? If they don't benefit directly
  will they do so indirectly (e.g. through capital and infrastructure
  projects, or through their contribution to other public services like
  health, justice and education)? In the UK, will the likely meltdown
  of the Public Finance Initiative (PFI – a scheme in which 'risk' is
  purportedly shared with the private sector, including now several
  banks with substantial public stakes), as well as an array of other
  joint ventures have a special effect? The omens are not good (BBC
  News Online 2009; Mathiason 2009).
- The third is about university–business interaction. Will industries
  invest in training and development through the slump, or not?
  Similarly, what will happen to commercial research and development (R&D)? Is it more or less likely to be shared with universities?
  What about the twenty-first century development of 'university-
  like businesses' (as discovered by Gary Hamel, and discussed further in Chapter 6) (Hamel 2007)?

- The fourth is about governance. Are we likely to see increased or reduced autonomy (not least in a context where university stewardship and risk-spreading – much criticized by the business establishment – has turned out to be rather sensible)?
- Connected with this, fifthly, are we likely to see more or less government intervention? I suspect that in many highly tinkered-with systems (like the UK and the Australian) the temptation will be to declare (temporarily) 'finished business' (as a euphemism for 'too hard').
- The sixth is about the 'for-profit' private competition for universities. Will these companies accelerate (to undercut the establishment) or decelerate (because entry and maintenance costs are so high)?
- The seventh is about staff. Will HE continue to be a public sector haven for professionals (with relatively safe pay and conditions, including vestigial pensions)? Will international mobility increase or decrease? Will competition for senior posts (including the VC pool) be boosted by corporate refugees? Will 'brain circulation' slow down? How many redundancies will there be? Will economic circumstances lead to consolidation or 'clearing-out' of subject and professional groups?
- The eighth is about national ambitions for HE. Will the race to a seriously brittle notion of 'world-classness' (discussed in Chapter 5) heat up or slow down (as the costs look more daunting and other priorities for HEIs loom larger)?
- The ninth is a sort of reciprocal of the eighth: will international cooperation (distinctly on the rise in research terms, if not on teaching and systems development) increase or decrease? As students have to stay at home, will there be re-focusing of 'first' and 'second' world effort away from a race to suck in international students and towards more traditional modes of development assistance for developing systems?
- The tenth and final fork sort of captures all of the options above. Will the sector draw in its horns, seek to ride out the difficulties and tend to close down, or will it take advantages of the elements of opportunity as opposed to threat in what's above, and open up? And what will be the resulting impact on university morale?

Much of the following material has been fermenting for me personally throughout a long career of being managed, of managing and (finally) of being managed again in HE. Authors often refer to topics that they tackle through a mixture of fear and fascination (see, e.g., Atwood 2008: 2). Studying my own tribe – the one among which I have lived and worked for my entire professional life – evokes both of these feelings. Indeed, I feel that this is the most personal of all of my books on HE. In this spirit I have included a dozen 'digressions' covering both direct experience of some of the issues raised and reflections from the 'hinterland'.

Some of it has appeared before, including in the pages of *The Times Higher Education Supplement* (*THES*) (and its successor, *Times Higher Education* [*THE*]), *Engage* (the magazine of the Leadership Foundation for Higher Education [LFHE]), *Perspectives: Policy and Practice in Higher Education* (from the Association of University Administrators [AUA]), the Quality Assurance Agency's (QAA) series *Quality Matters*, the *Higher Education Quarterly* and *Higher Education Review*. John Skelton of Open University Press and latterly Shona Mullen of McGraw-Hill have also proved wise, generous and supportive commissioning editors as I have worked through preliminary versions of many of the ideas here in a series of books.

This autobiographical flavour means that the bulk of the story concerns UK HE, in which I have worked consistently since 1975 (in four institutions). However, my other research interests have taken me elsewhere, especially to the USA, to Australia, to Ireland, and to China and Japan. Empirical judgements about other people's systems must always start from an appropriately humble standpoint. You have to live inside a system fully to understand it: a failing exhibited by many of the eminent Americans who have sought to explain UK HE from their perspective as guests at the Oxbridge High Table. But – as some of the material below indicates – I am sure that in several important respects we are not alone.

I am particularly thankful for the insights, guidance and constructive disagreement of friends and colleagues in a variety of settings. I am especially grateful to participants in seminars on the theme at Leeds Metropolitan University (September 2007), the Universities of Melbourne (August 2008) and Sydney (September 2008), and Queen Mary University of London (January 2009). As will be apparent, my dialogue with colleagues and students at the University of Brighton and (since 2005) on the MBA in Higher Education Management at the Institute of Education has been a source of consistent stimulation, and surprise. Individual readers of and commentators on some or all of what follows include Sharon Bell, Rachel Bowden, Denise Batchelor, David Halpin, David House, David Palfreyman, David Roberts, Peter Scott, Betty Skolnick and Paul Temple. Of course, they have not invariably agreed with me. However, a remarkable number of my friends and allies are not grumpy, in the collective sense alluded to above. Indeed my dedication is to two of the most inspiring anti-cynics – now sadly lost – both of whom I was proud to count as colleagues and friends, and with whom I am sad that I shall not be able to argue (as I am sure I would have), about what is in this book.

In my darker moments I think about what giving way to cynicism might mean. What if expecting 'mass' or 'universal' rates of HE participation to mean access for significantly more people to something that had been a severely rationed good is nothing more than a pipe dream (it won't work, and they couldn't handle it anyway)? Was Martin Trow (1989) right about this? What if the only decent research is in fact in the Russell Group, and Paul Wellings is right about that (and the consequence that, in terms of research activity, the best of what we have is the best we can ever hope for) (Fearn, 2008a)? What if the only thing that matters is where you go (as a student) or where you are (as a staff member), as apparently argued by the Sutton Trust (2008)? What if it is true that staff members are regularly bullied into giving higher marks than their students deserve so that their institutions can climb the league tables (as Geoffrey Alderman asserts on a regular basis – see his contribution to 'Can't think, won't think') (Alderman 2009)? What if businessmen (and women) really do always know better than academics how to run a university (as argued in central New Labour circles)? What if all VCs are egocentric bastards (as I have heard one former registrar – who will have to remain anonymous – argue strongly), or what if being a successful VC has nothing to do with remaining engaged with scholarly work (as suggested, in a more public and empirical fashion, by a current registrar) (Allen 2008)?

When I recover, I think not – to all of these questions. But am I falling between two stools? I like what mass HE has done for societies, and for the wider world. I take pleasure in the greater number of individuals whom it has forced to change themselves from the inside out. But I also think that what brings about this change (or, to use the jargon, this 'transformation') is rooted in some eternal verities: in a university mission, which we inherit, modify (and ideally make more fit for purpose in our own times) and then pass on. When that works, morale should be high enough. Most importantly, the people who I have come to admire, respect and emulate most in the system are emphatically not cynical (the same is true of the vast majority of the 100 voices introduced in Chapter 4). This book is intended to help to keep alight their optimistic candles.

2

HIGHER EDUCATION AND OUR PRESENT CONDITION

This chapter starts from a simple premise: that universities and colleges cannot escape the real world. They are of it, as well as in it, and their communities are no longer immune to its perils, vicissitudes and pleasures. One of these today is the barrage of injunctions from the happiness industry.

Happiness has become a publishing sensation of the early twenty-first century; not least because it is felt that it is something which we once had and have now lost: at home, at work, in community and national contexts, and in even more general senses.

The literature divides into some distinct genres:

- elegiac nostalgia;
- furious dystopianism;
- international competitiveness (to be either the best or the worst);
- radical therapeutics;
- critique of such therapeutics;
- popular self-help.

I attempt to treat at least some parts of this vast (and uneven) literature below, under three headings. The first is an exploration of the solutions proposed by the proponents of a new 'science of happiness' and the response of their critics. The result is, I believe, an unedifying stand-off between too simple an idea and too self-satisfied a critique. The second represents a wider and, in my view, more fruitful series of perspectives from social theory, literature and cultural activities in general, seeking to explore the spirit of our times. The third is specifically contemporary: HE's own version of the battle of the generations, especially as it is mediated by information and communications technology (ICT).

The science of happiness   ■

The prophet of a scientific solution to the social problem of unhappiness is the distinguished economist and educational theorist Richard Layard:

> Economics equates changes in the happiness of a society with changes in its purchasing power – or roughly so. I have never accepted that view, and the history of the last fifty years has disproved it. Instead, the new science of happiness makes it possible to construct an alternative view, based on evidence rather than assertion. From this we can develop a new vision of what lifestyles and what policies are sensible, drawing on the new psychology, as well as on economics, brain science, sociology and philosophy.
>
> (Layard 2005: ix; see also *The Economist*, 2006–7)

Layard has promoted this view vigorously across the media. This is from an interview in the *Guardian*:

> 'Happiness is inversely related to income at higher levels of income because of the declining marginal utility of getting richer,' says Layard. 'Let me show you.' He draws a graph: on the X axis is income per head, on the Y axis is average happiness. A curve ascends boldly and then tails off ignominiously. At the bottom of the curve you will find countries like Zimbabwe or Russia, where increases in national income will increase levels of happiness.
>
> (Jeffries 2008)

This is not a new insight. McMahon prints exactly this table, entitled 'subjective well-being by level of economic development' and derived from the World Bank Values Surveys published in 1997 (McMahon 2006: 468). Very similar points are made by the epidemiologist Michael Marmot and the social statisticians Richard Wilkinson and Kate Pickett (Marmot 2004; Wilkinson and Pickett 2009). Among the other contributions by economists has been the attempt to place monetary values on aspects of happiness by David Blanchflower (a member of the British Bank of England's Monetary

Policy Committee). Blanchflower has not been able to escape the notoriety of having once placed a value on a 'regular sex life' (it was $50,000 a year) (Pilkington 2008).

As for Layard's solution: '[i]n his ... The Depression Report he recommended scaling up CBT (Cognitive Behavioural Therapy) for people suffering from depression and anxiety through training an additional 10,000 clinical psychologists and psychological therapists' (Jeffries 2008).

In 2005–6 the most popular Harvard course was apparently a class in positive psychology taught by Tal Ben-Shahar, the former Israeli national squash champion (with 855 registrations it beat the staple 'Introduction to Economics' which had only 688) (see Ben-Shahar 2006, 2007a). Also in 2006 both Wellington College and the University of East London made headlines by beginning to teach 'happiness' (the latter offering an 'MSc in Applied Positive Psychology'). In September 2007 the Children's Secretary of State pledged £14 million over four years to extend the Social and Emotional Aspects of Learning (SEAL) programme from primary to secondary schools (Press Association, 4 September). In December 2008 Leeds Trinity and All Saints College announced a foundation degree in 'Workplace Well-being'. At the apex of the UK HE system, the University of Cambridge has launched the multi-disciplinary Cambridge Well-being Institute (see www.cambridgewellbeing.org).

Together these initiatives build on the pioneering work of Martin Seligman and a group of psychologists behind the Penn Resilience Program (PRP – see also www.authentichappiness.org). For this theory, the problems begin (with strong echoes of Layard) in the conditions of relative affluence by global standards and a plethora of choice. But the immediate pathologies are played out in adolescent depression, against which PRP (a mixture of CBT and social skills such as negotiation, coping strategies and decision-making) is a form of immunization (Bunting 2008; see also Halpern 2008).

There is also an emerging set of league tables ranking nations and groups according to their happiness: the happiest person to be is, apparently, a middle-aged Dutch woman (Brothers 2007). The New Economics Foundation (NEF) has worked with the Cambridge group (above) to generate what they call 'the most comprehensive international survey of well-being to date'. For the UK the results are not encouraging:

- The UK is ranked thirteenth, out of 22 European nations, when combining ratings for personal and social well-being, managing only fifteenth for social well-being and thirteenth for personal well-being alone.

- The UK fares particularly poorly compared to other Western European nations where we fall third from the bottom on both personal and social well-being.
- Although people in the UK are relatively satisfied with their lives, they score poorly on measures of vitality and sense of meaning and engagement.
- Denmark, Switzerland and Norway show the highest levels of overall well-being, while Central and Eastern European countries such as the Ukraine, Bulgaria and Hungary have the lowest (NEF 2009).

On a more popular level, in the *Geography of Bliss*, Eric Weiner (2008) sets out to find 'the world's happiest country'. This engaging book is actually a Bill Bryson-style guide to a related world of social scientific theory (the distribution of subjective well-being, as set out by today's academic gurus – Seligman, Veenhoven, Inglehart, McMahon, Layard, Schoch etc. – as well as their historical antecedents – Mill, Bentham, Schopenhauer, Nietzsche etc.) coupled with confessional tourism. The Rawlsian premise (following Ruud Veenhoven's World Database of Happiness in Rotterdam) is that 'the quality of the society is more important than your place in that society'. Or, as one of his interviewees (from Slough, England) put it, 'Look if you have something fundamentally shitty, you can't do much with it, can you?' (Weiner 2008: 278, 332). Weiner's hedonic winner is Iceland (he was writing before the country effectively went bankrupt in late 2008):

> ... a country that has no right to be happy and yet is. Iceland gets the balance right. A small country but a cosmopolitan one. Dark and light. Efficient and laid back. American gumption married to European social responsibility. A perfect, happy relationship. The glue which holds the whole enterprise together is culture. It makes all the difference.
>
> (Weiner 2008: 406)

In the popular media, the analogue is an epidemic of self-help list guides and 'steps' on how to be happy. To take just one example, here are Ben-Shahar's 'four ways:'

- give yourself the permission to be human;
- simplify your life;
- exercise regularly;
- focus on the positive.

And (unsaid), buy the book (Ben-Shahar 2007b). And another one is promised soon: (*The Pursuit of Perfect*), with another version of PRP ('permission to be human', 'reconstruction', and 'perspective') (Park 2009). We are in the same territory here as the government's commissioning from the New Economics Foundation (NEF) of a prescription of 'five-a-day' actions to promote mental health and well-being (GOS 2008):

- connect with friends, family, colleagues and neighbours;
- learn something new;
- be active;
- take notice;
- help friends and neighbours.

As Lucy Mangan of the *Guardian* observes (having tried them out):

It remains for all but a fortunate few – whom I suspect are quite happy enough already – essentially unworkable advice. You might as well instruct the nation to live in the 1950s: surely the last time there was any hope of living this way *en masse*.

(Mangan 2008)

A more subtle (and less hubristic) set of prescriptions structures Oliver James's *Affluenza* (2007). For him a personal 'virus' ('the placing of a high value on money, possessions, appearances [physical and social] and fame') has a conditioning social context; 'in a developed economy, rates of emotional distress (disturbances such as depression, anxiety and substance abuse) increase in direct proportion to the degree of social inequality' (James 2007: xiii, xviii). His conclusion is stark: 'Cards on the table, I contend that most emotional distress is best understood as a rational response to sick societies. Change those societies, and we will all be less distressed' (p. xx).

This is exactly the conclusion that the Government Office for Science's (GOS) 'Foresight' programme on mental capital and well-being couldn't quite bring itself to utter. There is nothing here about redistribution of wealth, or about how the incapacity benefit rolls were expanded in the 1980s in order to manipulate unemployment figures. There is however, plenty about intervening early to 'boost brain power', using cognitive science to establish secure 'biomarkers' for learning difficulties, tackling the scourge of mental ill health (while noting its frequent association with debt), maintaining learning throughout life, and responding to pressure within the workplace. The basic argument is that the two concepts are 'intimately linked'. Mental capital's focus is on 'cognitive and emotional resources'. Meanwhile, mental well-being refers to a 'dynamic state' in which individuals are able to 'develop their potential, work productively and creatively, build strong and positive relationships with others and contribute to their community' (Beddington *et al.* 2008).

For a powerful (even rabble-rousing) critique of such interventions through the education system see Ecclestone (2007): 'vast numbers of experts are attending to the psychological wellbeing of students. But there's no proof they're doing the slightest good'. As for adults – away from the clutches of schools, colleges and universities – John Cloud reports on work in the USA that suggests we are colluding: 'we now have a "legal drug culture" built around the widely accepted idea that feeling blue is an illness ... that 'many instances of normal sadness are now diagnosed as depressive disorder' (Cloud 2007; see also Crews 2007).

Some critics are even more forthright about the right to unhappiness. Sue Halpern summarizes Eric Wilson's diatribe, *Against Happiness: In Praise of Melancholy* (2008), as 'an inventory of complaints about people who pursue happiness as a vocation, a birthright, or both':

> They're deluded he says, unrealistic, inauthentic. They fail to acknowledge the misery in the world and live in emotionally gated communities. Their intentional obtuseness is the cause of cultural vapidity, environmental destruction, blandness, cupidity. Better to be 'born to the blues,' as he declares, and experience the world in all its dimensions.
>
> (Halpern 2008: 26)

Respected social scientists concur. A group of American therapists, reporting in the *Journal of Marital and Family Therapy*, have attacked 'cultural fairytales and modern love stories for perpetuating the myth that enjoying a perfect relationship is possible'. Diane Gehart and Eric McCollum say that it's a myth (perpetuated by the very concept of mental health) that 'with enough effort we can achieve a state without suffering' (BBC News Online 2008a). Frederick Crews, reporting on a series of critical books on the mass prescription of antidepressants describes 'a demonstration that episodic sadness has always been a socially approved means of adjusting to misfortune, and that much is lost, both medically and culturally, when it is misread as a depressive disorder' (Crews 2007: 14). The anthropologist Amy Pollard has conducted what she calls an 'opportunistic' study of people who are happy and over 50. Its conclusions are similarly nuanced: 'With so many different kinds of happiness available in the world, there are also many different ways to reach it' (Pollard 2008: 2).

Cognitive behavioural therapy (CBT) has attracted a broad range of principled critique, not least because of its quick-fix characteristics. Darian Leader, for example, sees it as 'a grotesque new mis-understanding of psychotherapy', a product of 'the commodification of the psyche':

> The divided self dear to the 60s has vanished, along with the recognition that grief, despair and frustration strike at the heart of our image of self-possession and fulfilment. The psyche has become like a muscle that needs to be developed and trained. There is no place for complexity and contradiction here: the modern subject is represented as one-dimensional, searching for fulfilment. The possibility that human life is aimed at both success and failure and never simply at wealth, power and happiness no longer makes sense. Suddenly the world of human relations described by novelists, poets and playwrights for the past few centuries can just be written off. Self-sabotage, masochism and despair are now faults to be corrected, rather than forming the very core of the self.
>
> (Leader 2008)

Perhaps there should be a right to unhappiness, or at least a 'conscience clause' to opt out of officially prescribed happiness. In the word of John Stuart Mill: 'ask yourself whether you are happy and you cease to be so' (quoted in Weiner 2008: 103–4).

An unhappy land: social change and the mood of the times ∎

Behind what Weiner calls 'the self-help industrial complex' lies a much more profound corpus of social and political thought. It has several disciplinary roots.

Part of it is historical and philosophical, as in the work of Richard Schoch or Jonathan Haidt (Haidt 2006; Schoch 2006):

> We have lost contact with the old and rich traditions of happiness, and we have lost the ability to understand their essentially moral nature. Deaf to the wisdom of the ages, we deny ourselves the chance of finding a happiness that is meaningful. We've settled, nowadays for a much weaker, much thinner, happiness: mere enjoyment of pleasure, mere avoidance of pain and

suffering. Somewhere between Plato and Prozac, happiness stopped being a lofty achievement and became an entitlement.

(Schoch 2006: 1)

Literature has a role to play too. Here is Sue Townsend, whose social critique at times approaches the incisiveness of George Orwell (her analysis almost exactly anticipates that of Zygmunt Bauman in his *Art of Life*) (Bauman 2008: 8–14).

> England was an unhappy land. The people were fearful, believing that life itself was composed of danger, and unknown and unknowable threats to their safety. Old people did not leave their houses after dark, children were not allowed to play outside even in the day-light hours and were escorted everywhere by anxious adults. To make themselves feel better the people spent their money on things that diverted and amused them. There was always something they thought they must have to make themselves happy. But when they had bought the object of their desire they found to their profound disappointment that the object was no longer desirable, and that far from making them happy, they felt nothing but remorse and the sadness of loss ...
>
> (Townsend, 2006: 11)

Sociologically, youth in particular is in the dock. A *Time* report from early 2008 concluded that 'an epidemic of violent crime, teen pregnancy, heavy drinking and drug abuse fuels fears that British youth is in crisis' (Mayer 2008). Meanwhile the Rowntree Foundation has consulted widely on views about contemporary social evils. Most of these seem to be much more individualistic than those famously trumpeted by Beveridge for attention in the post-war world, or even Joseph Rowntree himself in 1904:

> A particularly dominant theme concerned the distinct but connected issues of *individualism, consumerism and greed, and a decline of community*. Participants felt that values rooted in relationships and communities have been eclipsed by a concern only for ourselves, our immediate family and consumer goods.
>
> (Watts 2008: 3)

Joseph Rowntree's 'major social ills' had been poverty, war, slavery, intemperance, the opium trade, impurity and gambling. What has really changed, except the technical indicators and their intensity?

The educational critique has been most fully (some would say over-) extended in *The Dangerous Rise of Therapeutic Education* by Katherine

Ecclestone and Dennis Hayes. In their view, current 'populist or-
thodoxies reflect and reinforce the concept of a diminished self'
(Ecclestone and Hayes 2009: xi). The charge is severe:

> The celebration of the emotional over the intellectual funda-
> mentally alters the historical idea of what it is to be human. Far
> from creating a more balanced and rounded personality, ther-
> apeutic education promotes the emotionally diminished subject
> and promote [sic] a life focused on the self and self-fulfilment
> rather than with understanding and changing the world.
> (Ecclestone and Hayes 2009: 164)

Across the educational system, we are apparently all to blame, as
Ecclestone and Hayes march their reader through the 'therapeutic'
variants of the primary school, secondary school, further education
(FE) college, university and workplace. To pause (for obvious reasons)
on the 'therapeutic university', this monstrosity is an 'emotional
treadmill', raising the question of 'what has happened to the life of
the mind to make it an emotional rather than a critical business'. It
works its wickedness by 'infantilizing students' (those declaring
themselves dyslexic come in for particular attack), through 'ubiquitous counselling' courses (like Ben-Shahar's) on 'emotional intelligence, emotional literacy, and emotional well-being', and the
weakening of academic freedom by reducing 'the expression of ideas
to the expression of emotion' (or at least seeing them as 'equally
important'). Particularly in the dock are the HE philosophers Ron
Barnett, Bruce Macfarlane and Stephen Rowland. As a consequence
of interventions by them and others, we have lost the sense of HE as
a necessary cold bath: either avoiding 'going the hard way' (in the
words of Wittgenstein) or failing to practise 'the denial of self in the
pursuit of knowledge' (Ecclestone and Hayes 2009: 86–104).
A more nuanced educational critique comes from the psy-
chotherapist Adam Phillips (2008: 46). He begins with what he calls a
'few obvious truths':

> First that cruelty makes some people happy, and makes most
> people happy at least sometimes. Second, that it is not clear that
> the pursuit of happiness necessarily brings out the best in peo-
> ple; people can do terrible things as a means to the end of
> happiness. Indeed the pursuit of happiness can make people
> immoral. And third, and most obvious, that what makes people
> happy is often very idiosyncratic, very personal and sometimes
> private.

Echoing Wilson and Leader, Phillips suggests that 'happiness as a moral demand – you must be happy, and you are failing if you are not – is pernicious'. This leads on to a much more subtle charge to the educational system, especially in school, where many pupils experience their first social group outside the family: 'it should at least show you the forms that happiness can take and that you can't get from your family'. This is a considerably more nuanced proposition than universal CBT: 'It may be best to end up saying something like: education should be showing children good ways of bearing their unhappiness, and good ways of taking their happiness when it comes (Phillips 2008: 47, 49).

Several broader contemporary developments are relevant here. The first batch concerns changes in legal and other frameworks and their implications. This has led to a general cultural increase in resort to formal complaint, and to litigation. One outcome of unhappiness is a culture of complaint (Baggini 2008). Julian Baggini's own complaint (in his book of that title) is that a noble tradition has been degraded.

> At its noblest, complaint – as a directed expression of refusal or inability to accept that things are not as they ought to be – lies at the heart of all campaigns to create a better, more just world. At its worst complaint is manifest in a grievance culture, which undermines ethics and replaces it with a legislative set of attitudes which undermine responsibility, freedom and a proper sense of life's contingencies.
>
> (Baggini 2008: 127)

A second group of commentators is more philosophical. It could be termed the solipsistic (some, following Christopher Lasch, say narcissistic) turn in contemporary social thought (Lasch 1984). Weiner, for example, is convinced that happiness has to be 'relational': 'The axiom of the self-help industrial complex is so ingrained as to be self-evident. There's only one problem: it's not true. Happiness is not inside us but out there. Or to be more precise, the line between out there and in here is not as sharply defined as we think' (Weiner 2008: 15).

For Andrew Marr, the *History of Modern Britain* is 'the story of the defeat of politics by shopping' (Marr 2007: 97). As Townsend (above) reflects, this has not necessarily made us happier, while Jonathan Guthrie (the 'enterprise editor' of the *Financial Times*) suggests, nor should it: 'Well-being economists, who study the influence of money on happiness, say that stagnant and declining earnings do not make people particularly miserable. Shopping does not improve wellbeing, so switching to a low-consumption life-style does not impair it much either' (Guthrie 2008: 25).

For the historian Barbara Ehrenreich, the rot set in long ago, as a result of Calvinism and the decline of collective joy (Ehrenreich 2007); for other academic treatments of the combination of consumption and discontent see Easterbrook (2003) and McMahon (2006).

For the pharmacologist and neuroscientist Susan Greenfield, the ways in which we use ICT are largely to blame. The outcome is a negative development in the ways in which we use our brains:

> The new technologies are so invasive because interacting with the screen and doing so in a solitary way mandates you living in two dimensions ... Human beings always listened to stories and had long working memories. Now it's action, reaction, action reaction ... You focus on the process. The experience offered by a computer is the excitement of an anticipated reward. And frustration if you don't get it. In neurochemical terms it's very similar to when you take a drug ... Up till now [pleasure-seeking] has always been part of our lives, but a polar opposite to seeking meaning. I fear we are shifting too much in favour of the literal, the hedonistic, the here and now, and losing meaning, context and content in favour of process.
>
> (Moreton 2008)

Finally we need to go down the political road. A particular moral panic was sparked by the United Nations Children's Fund (UNICEF) 2007 report placing British children at the bottom of a league table on happiness and well-being. Using 40 indicators from the period 2000–3 (like poverty, family relationships and health) the UK was at the foot of the 21-country table, one below the USA (again the Netherlands came top, ahead of – in order – Sweden, Denmark and Finland) (BBC News Online 2007). A certain amount of data war has sprung up about the findings, but the main political and professional response has been of grudging acknowledgement of a serious problem. Together these elements have each contributed to a political concern – by all of the major UK parties – with what they call 'well-being'.

In early 2009 the UNICEF report was followed by the publication of the results of a three-year inquiry by the Children's Society. The principal finding echoes that of the Rowntree Foundation – most problems can be traced back to adult selfishness:

> But most of all our adult society has to change. For in the end the values which children will absorb will be the values of the

society around them. In recent years traditional beliefs have weakened and the void has been filled by an excessive individualism, which holds that our main duty is to make the most of ourselves. Too often, this means being as successful as possible, in what becomes a struggle of each against all.

(Layard and Dunn 2009: 162)

Interestingly, Layard uses his joint authorship of the report to push another platform for CBT. While the system of National Curriculum tests should be swept away, it would 'help if schools administered *standard assessments of emotional and behavioural well-being* to all students at 5, 11 (in primary school) and 14' (Layard and Dunn 2009: 158).

Generational fracture

Educationally, what may be most important, at least temporarily, is generational tension between students and many of their teachers (Heller and d'Ambrosio 2008). Johanna Wyn lists some of our feebler attempts to articulate what is happening to the generation behind us: 'post-adolescence', 'generation on hold', 'generations X, Y and Z' and 'arrested adulthood'. However, her central insight is that an earlier sense of adulthood has gone, and that we are in the midst of a new 'invention of adulthood' (Wyn 2008). The outcome is a revised dialectic of dependence and independence. There is the paradox of growing up both faster and more slowly.

In the West, the hinge of adulthood appears to be stabilizing around the mid-twenties. The resulting elongated dependence (both financial and emotional) causes tensions in both directions. 'Helicopter parents' can find that after not very long they are saddled with 'boomerang kids' (Acocella 2008: 102; Koss-Feder 2009). The resulting generational fracture has a number of interrelated dimensions.

Most frequently it is seen as being about ICT: not just the kit, but also an attitude of mind. Students – as young adults – live in a different world to many of their teachers. They have what Jason Frand calls 'the information age mind-set' (Frand 2000) and they attend what Tara Brabazon memorably calls the 'university of google' (Brabazon 2007).

Brabazon's is an *urtext* of the tendency described in the next chapter as academic condescension. She writes eloquently about the need for an 'information scaffold', for 'slow reading' and for moving from 'a cultural to a critical literacy', but her methods are fiercely didactic and the general effect is brittle and polemical. She describes heroic personal over-working, students who are either fawningly grateful or feckless, ubiquitously bankrupt university leadership, and invariably inefficient and inadequate administrative and technical support. Her fundamental message is generational:

> We had to work it out for ourselves. It was an environment of fear: a fear of failure. At the very time that capitalism was benevolent, the university system was preparing us for the ruthless inequalities we would confront upon leaving a leafy campus.
> Now that there are wars on terror, casualized workplaces, little union protection for workers and an economy based on credit card debt, universities are soft but cuddly institutions, shielding our students from the dire reality of life.
>
> (Brabazon 2007: 125)

Frand's formulation – now almost a decade old – is much more subtle and respectful of change. He describes 10 features of a world inhabited and managed by students who have grown up with the personal computer, the worldwide web and the mobile phone. The full list is as follows:

- computers aren't technology;
- internet better than TV;
- reality no longer real;
- doing rather than knowing;
- Nintendo over logic;
- multitasking way of life;
- typing rather than handwriting;
- staying connected;
- zero tolerance for delays;
- consumer/creator blurring.

Most of these are blindingly obvious to anyone who lives with or around young adults (the torture of using a pen for just the two weeks of the examination season, the surgically attached mobile phone, the conversation that takes place simultaneously with text messaging, the death of the instruction manual), but at least two are of profound significance for the pedagogical enterprise. You learn from a computer game by endless failing (and trying – following the Samuel Beckett injunction to 'fail better') and you create (legitimately) by sampling, quoting and manipulating (as on Photoshop, say, or Sibelius). In 2008 the market for video games overtook those for books and music and DVDs (John Lanchester calculates the three markets as £4.64 billion, £4.46 and £4.1 billion respectively) (Lanchester 2009).

Frand spotted the moment when young people moved from TV to the internet. However, he was in advance of their latest move: from the computer to telephony. For example, the latest rage in Japan is the *keitai sho-setsu* or cell-phone novel, written by angst-written teenagers for their peers (Goodyear 2008), while the London-based girl band The Mentalists perform on iPhones (Prigg 2009).

This new world is what the TLRP calls Web 2.0: 'an umbrella term for a host of recent internet applications such as social networking, wikis, folksonomies, virtual societies, blogging, multiplayer online gaming and mash-ups' (TLRP 2008: 4). In contrast, these students' teachers are predominantly occupants of what Richard Ford's Frank Bascombe calls in *The Lay of the Land* (Ford 2006) – 'the Permanent Period', where life is a 'destination and no longer a journey'; see also Aspden (2007) on the travails of late middle age. In the face of the new technologies, student over-confidence can meet the teacher's lack of confidence (or worse, indifference). In particular, the older generation finds it hard to process the truncated extremes in which its successor expresses opinions using these highly fragmented media, whether as critique of individual lecturers or how the campus looks on open days. Peers will understand and aim off for the hyperbole (K. Smith 2008). Meanwhile, time marches on, and of course this state of affairs will not last: sooner rather than later the 'screenagers' will get to teach (for what then happens, see Levinson 2007).

In a further elaboration of this picture, Donald Heller and his collaborators, in a seminar on 'Generational Shockwaves and the Implications for Higher Education' (ironically part of a series sponsored by one of the leading providers of HE teachers' retirement funds), offer a three-way split: the 'Baby Boomers … born as World War II was coming to a close' and now 'near retirement'; 'Generation X … born largely in the 1960s and 1970s', many of whom have become the younger cohort of faculty who are now helping to teach the Millennial Generation of students, those born 'since 1980' (Heller and d'Ambrosio 2008: 1).

All of this is also about political generations. The older generation has confused indifference to their way of changing the world (significantly through party-political campaigning) with indifference in general. In fact (as discussed in the next chapter) the current generation of students is at least as idealistic as any of their predecessors: they are just more likely to express solidarity through international and ecological commitments. From this emanates different forms of mutuality and connectedness: more about families (with whom in the West they now remain intimately involved for longer – including for economic reasons) and friends, than organizations. It also involves different ways of scanning the horizon: not just for productive employment, but also in terms of the rewards it might bring, where the sense of personal entitlement (e.g. to status – or even to a pension) has receded.

Debt is a deeply symbolic issue between the generations, and another source of moral panic. As a translatlantic commentator observes, '[s]ince many younger Britons have never lived through a period of slower growth, few now see the need to hold back on borrowing, not to mention saving' (Werdiger 2008).

Western cultural attitudes towards financial debt have gone through both long-term and short-term cycles. On the longer scale there is the classic association between the Protestant Reformation and the rise of capitalism agonized over by Marxist and non-Marxist historians. In the shorter scheme of things there is the oscillation between a general cultural assumption that a certain level of personal and corporate debt is a good thing – fuelling the wheels of the economy; or a bad thing – representing a moral and socioeconomic trap. For most of the nineteenth century and well into the twentieth the latter was the basic assumption. Margaret Atwood argues brilliantly how the nineteenth-century novel was 'driven by money': 'the best nineteenth century revenge is not seeing your enemy's red blood all over the floor but seeing the red ink all over his balance sheet' (Atwood 2008: 100). The latter part of the twentieth century and the very beginning of the twenty-first reversed the field, at least until what is not (yet) called The Great Crash of 2008. The pyramidal structure of 'sub-prime mortgages', derivatives, leverage, arbitrage, private equity and hedge funds that finally imploded in this year not only validated the classic phrase of Gordon Gekko in the film *Wall Street* that 'greed is good' but also the heart of the curriculum of the Harvard MBA. As its most celebrated mole reported (before the Crash), according to the Harvard Business School (HBS), 'these days debt is good' (Broughton 2008: 109).

But perhaps the worm was turning before the Crash, unbeknown to the HBS (which is not good at futurology – one of the most entertaining parts of Broughton's insider story is the overnight curricular transformation of Jeffrey Skilling of Enron from hero to villain) (Broughton 2008: 157). According to Atwood's *Payback*, 'we seem to be entering a period in which debt has passed through its most recent harmless and fashionable period, and is reverting to being sinful'. She reports a friend as saying 'debt is the new fat' (Atwood 2008: 41).

Student bodies caught the wave, and may be left up the beach.

According to Atwood again: 'I'm told that university students tell tales about their ballooning student loans with rueful grins rather than with floods of despairing tears. Everyone's in debt – so what? That's the way it is, and how else are they supposed to get through school? As for paying it all off, they'll think about that later' (Atwood 2008: 131).

All of this raises the fundamental question of when genuine adulthood begins in developed societies in the early twenty-first century. The Inquiry into the Future of Lifelong Learning (IFLL) has been modelling a new approach to life stages in which a key transition occurs around 25 (the next staging posts appear to be around 50, when many begin to adjust their work patterns, and around 75, when modern 'older age' education seems to begin). The director of the IFLL, Tom Schuller, explains:

> Here is a radical suggestion, which would cut through some of the problems. The age at which most people in the UK – bar a few doctoral students – have finished their initial education is 25. Most finish well before, and some of these have already re-entered the education system. But 25 is a pretty good cut-off point – better anyway than 16, 18 or 21 … Other factors also speak in favour. Neuroscience tells us that the physical brain matures around the age of 25. It's the age at which many young people who engage in crime grow beyond their criminal activity, and we could do with a clearer transition bridge for them to find their way back into education and work. In short, it's roughly the age when young people more or less settle into a more stable pattern of life, professionally and personally, having explored various identities and various parts of the world.
>
> (Schuller 2008: 2)

The IFLL has built on this work to suggest 'four stages' of the learning life: 0–25, 25–50, 50–75 and 75+. In contrast, the Economic and Social Research Council (ESRC)-supported 'Tomorrow Group' elaborates (not quite following Shakespeare) 'seven stages:' 'birth, childhood, becoming an adult, personal relationships between roughly age 25 and 45, the middle years, retirement, and being very old' (Moynagh and Worsley 2009: 1–6).

From the HE perspective, as subsequent chapters will demonstrate, generational fracture in HE can occur along various dimensions:

- between students (in general) and staff (in general);
- between younger and older students;
- between younger and older staff (in general);

- between younger and older academic staff;
- between younger and older support staff;
- between younger academic and older support staff (and vice versa).

Sometimes unexpected coalitions and antipathies can thus be formed. Collusion (e.g. between students and staff against university leadership, or between university leadership and students against staff) can operate alongside simple bewilderment at what groups can and cannot do on either side of a generational divide. To take the famous complaint by employers about what job applicants (notably graduates) cannot do, it is interesting that there is a generational angle here too. The Learning and Skills Network (LSN) engaged in an interesting dialogue with 1137 employers about what exactly they meant. They found yet another 'generational divide': 'The age of the recruiter came through as a key factor. Younger respondents were more prepared to employ school or college leavers and therefore had much less difficulty in filling job vacancies. Older recruiters found it much more difficult to buy into what school or college leavers had to offer' (Lanning *et al.* 2008: 1–2).

It would be interesting to repeat this exercise at the graduate level.

Digression 1: parents and children

Generational fracture does not only occur between teachers and students. Parents and children are capable of giving each other similar grief, and the pattern recurs. The relationship under most pressure as a result of simultaneous arrested and accelerated adulthood is that between parents and children. The dimensions are manifold: emotional, economic, cultural and demographic.

Reading the account of Arthur and Dorothea Ponsonby's relationship with their daughter Elizabeth and her reprobate husband Dennis Pelly in D.J. Taylor's account of the 'bright young people' of the 1920s and 1930s is spookily reminiscent of the tabloid and free paper sagas of the party set of today's young London celebrities (an example is the coverage of the singer Amy Winehouse, her taxi driver cum radio personality dad Mitch, and her convicted husband, Blake Fielder-Civil (at the time of writing she has just sued for divorce). Only the geography has contracted. It is:

A world of whistle-stop journeys through Home Counties' back lanes, frenzied telephone calling and constant changes of plan, all-day drinking and physical exhaustion, dominated by the search for novelty: the latest fashionable restaurant, the newest Thames-side resort
(Taylor 2007: 104–5)

Ponsonby's political career was stellar. A former diplomat, as an MP he became a Liberal convert to Labour, rising to lead the Labour Party in the House of Lords (as 1st Baron Ponsonby of Shulbrede) between 1931 and 1935. A prominent peace activist (as he had been in World War I) he resigned from the Labour Party over its support for Churchill's coalition in 1940. As Taylor shows, however, his personal and emotional life – and that of Dorothea – was permanently and agonizingly tied up in the affairs of their daughter, who predeceased them both in July 1940 (she died of alcoholic poisoning). They had alternately financed (sometimes without each others' knowledge) and criticized her lifestyle and her relationships, as one of the brightest tabloid stars of the day. As Arthur (who it is rumoured wrote her otherwise surprisingly generous *Times* obituary himself), confided to her final employer: 'she lived in a world of which I knew nothing' (Taylor 2007: 271–2).

Parents may disapprove, but they can't let go.

The happiness industry relates to HE in some interesting ways. Happiness has invaded the institutions (including in curricular terms). 'Happiness' has been criticized by representatives of HE. More constructively, HE provides a fertile ground for testing the key hypotheses and intentions of the advocates of happiness as a panacea. Ultimately, I believe, higher education has played its role in exposing a false prospectus.

3

UNHAPPY STUDENTS

This chapter examines the contemporary situation of the student estate. In the UK, students' collective morale has rarely been considered systematically. In particular, questions are raised here about whether students in HE are primarily consumers, members or 'soft citizens'.

The student estate

In so far as mass HE in the UK has been a success, this is very significantly down to our students (Watson 2007c). The policy framework has contributed (often uneasily), the institutions and their staff have coped remarkably with the consequences of unfunded expansion, but on the key indicators – of matriculation, of retention (or what the Americans call more evocatively 'persistence'), of graduation and of postgraduate employment – the responsibility is theirs. This generation of students works extraordinarily hard (academically as well as to support their living and lifestyles); it cares as strongly as any of its predecessors for issues of justice and fairness (although it is much more likely to express these values in terms of environmental sustainability and global responsibility than through party politics); and it knows that the world does not owe it a living (as many felt that it did when only around 10 per cent of each age cohort had a higher level of education). One powerful, but counterintuitive, development is the revival – around the world – of student volunteering (Spanier 2008).

Students have also moulded the system in striking ways. This is partly about choice of subjects, where the reports have underlined the difficulties providers have faced (more successfully in recent years) in adjusting to the popularity and unpopularity of certain courses. The 'media studies' vogue, in a deeply ironic way, was a *demand*-led phenomenon (it's ironic, because one of the chief charges from the political-industrial complex is that HE doesn't respond to demand). Young people spotted the opportunities, in career as well as academic terms, of a studying a combination of ICT applications, design, promotion and marketing, as well as their relevance to particular subject and professional fields in a way that has eluded many of the critics; and they have been proved right. Media studies students do not all want to run the BBC.

Student choice is also about mode of study, where the sectoral supertanker has to deal with rapid growth in demand for part-time undergraduate and full-time postgraduate courses. It is about brands, where, for example, only in relation to the supply-led public service do Foundation Degrees seem to have high volume future prospects (see Chapter 5, Digression 6).

Finally, it is about choice of institutions. 'Hard to reach' groups remain concentrated in one particular part of the sector (normally the former 'public sector' institutions that were polytechnics, large colleges under local authority control and Scottish central institutions). However, contrary to the propaganda of some groups (like the Sutton Trust, which campaigns to get well-qualified 'non-standard' students into a small group of 'top' universities, and which sees this as a 'waste of talent'), their choices are not necessarily irrational (Sutton Trust 2008). There may be economic, familial and cultural reasons for wanting to study closer to home. There may be courses on offer which are perceived to be more attractive (especially those that relate to health, service and cultural professions) and the teaching styles may be felt to be more appropriate in the so-called 'new' universities. The Higher Education Policy Institute (HEPI) has pointed to the greater frequency of contact with mainstream academic staff in these institutions (as opposed to with research and teaching assistants), and there is some evidence of greater attention to pedagogical practice (Sastry and Bekhradnia 2007). To quote the TLRP's project on the Social and Organisational Mediation of University Learning (SOMUL), 'the amount of learning is not related to "quality" rankings of institutions (you won't necessarily learn more if you go to a posh place)' (SOMUL 2005).

There are further pedagogical implications. We have plenty of nostalgic and ideologically loaded analysis of what new and graduating students *can't* do; but there's precious little account taken of what today's screenagers *can* do – that many of their predecessors and at least some of their teachers can't. Most of this has to do with ICT and with the learning styles of what Jason Frand memorably calls 'the information-age mind-set' (discussed at the end of Chapter 2: see Frand 2000).

In these circumstances, the most important trap to avoid is that of condescension. Many institutions, course teams and individual teachers have responded positively to these elements of co-production. Others have reacted much more negatively. See for example, Robert Stevens' Oxford-based attack on mass HE (Stephens 2004), Mary Evans' identification of quality audit and assessment with the officials of the Third Reich (Evans 2004) and Frank Furedi's lament for the loss of cultural authority (Furedi 2004). Furedi is disappointed by everything: by his students, by his 'employers' the university, by his loss of status and authority, by most aspects of popular culture, by almost everything technology has done to his mode of production, and by the apparent death of the Enlightenment project.

As far as staff–student relationships are concerned, the outcome is often a toxic combination of such condescension and dismissal. This is Ted Gup, a professor of journalism at Case Western Reserve University, reporting on his experience:

> In recent years I have administered a dumbed-down quiz on current events and history early in each semester to get a sense of what my students know and don't know. Initially I worried that its simplicity would insult them, but my fears were unfounded. The results have been, well, horrifying.
>
> Nearly half of a recent class could not name a single country that bordered Israel. In an introductory journalism class, 11 of 18 students could not name what country Kabul was in, although we have been at war there for half a decade. Last fall only one in 21 students could name the U.S. secretary of defense. Given a list of four countries – China, Cuba, India and Japan – not one of those same 21 students could identify India and Japan as democracies. Their grasp of history was little better. The question of when the Civil War was fought invited an array of responses – half a dozen were off by a decade or more. Some students thought that Islam was the principal religion of South America, that Roe vs. Wade was about slavery, that 50 judges sit on the U.S. Supreme Court, that the atom bomb was dropped on Hiroshima in 1975. You get the picture, and it isn't pretty.
>
> (Gup 2008)

There are at least two types of American reaction to this sort of diatribe. The first is to point out that elders are not necessarily any better. The American Civic Literacy Program, organized by the

Intercollegiate Studies Institute (ISI), regularly tests the general public, with depressing results:

> More than 2,500 randomly selected Americans took ISI's basic 33-question test on civic literacy and more than 1,700 people failed, with the average score 49 percent, or an 'F.' Elected officials scored even lower than the general public with an average score of 44 percent and only 0.8 percent (or 21) of all surveyed earned an 'A.'

For the ISI, both 'the blame and the solution … lie at the doorstep of the nation's colleges' (ISI 2008). (Before we feel any sense of British superiority, a survey of 2,060 'representative adults' to celebrate the 200th anniversary of Charles Darwin's birth revealed that 5 per cent thought the great man wrote *A Brief History of Time*, 3 per cent *The God Delusion*, and 1 per cent *The Naked Chef*; see www.guardian. co.uk/science/charles-darwin.

The second possible response is the grudging acceptance that there may be some things which today's students do better. For example, Thomas H. Bender, reviewing a slew of books in this mode for the *Chronicle of Higher Education*, begins by reflecting on how much they confirm his everyday experience as a college teacher:

> I see too many students who are:

- Primarily focused on their own emotions—on the primacy of their 'feelings'—rather than on analysis supported by evidence.
- Uncertain what constitutes reliable evidence, thus tending to use the most easily found sources uncritically.
- Convinced that no opinion is worth more than another: All views are equal.
- Uncertain about academic honesty and what constitutes plagiarism. (I recently had a student defend herself by claiming that her paper was more than 50 percent original, so she should receive that much credit, at least.)
- Unable to follow or make a sustained argument.
- Uncertain about spelling and punctuation (and skeptical that such skills matter).
- Hostile to anything that is not directly relevant to their career goals, which are vaguely understood.
- Increasingly interested in the social and athletic above the academic, while 'needing' to receive very high grades.
- Not really embarrassed at their lack of knowledge and skills.

- Certain that any academic failure is the fault of the professor rather than the student.

However, Bender goes on:

> On the other hand, I am not so pessimistic about the abilities of the 'digital natives.' Different generations have different ways of knowing—different configurations of multiple intelligences. Pick your era and your subject: How many of us know anything about farming anymore or how to read the changing of the seasons? How many of us know how to repair an automobile or make a cake from scratch?
>
> Of course, we lament that the skills we have acquired at great pains can become lost to the next generation, but we can hardly reverse all of it. And it may be that the young are better adapted to what is coming than we are.
>
> (Bender 2008)

This is where the critique of student instrumentalism comes in, and the suggestion that students have shifted from being members of an academic community to simple consumers of an academic product. Students certainly know that credentialism counts: it is one of the prices of a larger, fairer system. But they also know that they are not in the business of simply purchasing a degree. Look at all of the evidence from student surveys. What do they want the 'new' fee income spent on? More and better library and computing resources and staff development in support of teaching (see Bekhradnia *et al.* 2006: 8). What do they most value in the teaching relationship (as revealed in the National Student Survey [NSS], discussed below)? Old-fashioned formative feedback on how they are doing.

Ron Barnett's *A Will to Learn* is a principled and eloquent reminder of some of these timeless verities. For him 'the inspirational teacher gives the student more than the teacher can himself control or even understand', while an effective pedagogy will challenge a student's existential being: 'she wills herself to go forward into those spaces which may well challenge her being itself'. For him: 'This is not fantasy. It is achieved day in and day out, even in mass higher education, and even against the odds' (Barnett 2007: 116, 155, 165).

The global campus

What binds the student community together in these new(ish) social conditions?

Probably most important is the fact that the university campuses in the UK (and I suspect in some other countries) are ahead of the wider community in demonstrating ethnic, cultural and national diversity. In the UK at present a majority of HEIs now have students from over 100 countries and several have a majority who are bilingual. One of Paul Ramsden's key pieces of advice to the Secretary of State (see below) is to institute 'intercultural fluency' as a 'central goal of every higher education curriculum' (Ramsden 2008: 3.14). Universities that do this will often find that they are following – not leading – their student bodies.

There is a romantic history of undergraduate student protest, which is not all fiction. Think of the members of the Oxford Union in 1933 deciding that they would prefer not to fight for king and country. And think of the global movement that closed universities in 1968. In England, two subsequent ministers of HE were prominent on the barricades: Kim Howells at Hornsey School of Art and Tessa Blackstone at the LSE (Jack Straw – now Secretary of State for Justice – was President of the National Union of Students [NUS]). In Cambridge, undergraduates were sent to prison for 6–12 months by Justice Melford Stevenson for their role in the riot at the Garden House Hotel in February 1970 (he implied that the sentence would have been harsher but for the effect on their impressionable minds of some of their radical tutors) (Crook 2006). Also in 1970, 13 students protesting the bombing of Cambodia were shot at Kent State University by members of the Ohio National Guard; four died. In 1986 – following a long student campaign – Barclays Bank was compelled to shut down its business in South Africa. Passions were overtly political, as were aims and presumed remedies.

Forty years on, the only whiff of cordite or the petrol bomb is in countries like Greece, where universities maintain their role not only as key components in a radical alliance but also as constitutionally guaranteed refuges; or Thailand, where the student vote is critical in a fragile democracy; or France, where student and staff bodies are aligned firmly with the defence of workers' rights (Bintliff 2009). In general, western student protest appears to have been snuffed out or replaced by a series of concerns over finance, hygiene factors (like facilities and accommodation) or the market-place currency of qualifications. The NUS can still mobilize demonstrations about the costs of HE and who should meet them; there has been a smattering of 'rent-strike'-style actions over campus services; campus security is an issue on both inner-city and some rural campuses; and any apparent threat to the professional recognition of courses prompts an immediate reaction. Passion, it seems, has become self-interested and tactical rather than principled.

In my view both of these images are overdrawn. The sixties heyday had its self-indulgent edges and something of a soft centre. The contemporary student scene can be just as committed and energetic. In early 2009, 'sit-ins' have returned in the UK: over the issue of Israel's action in the Gaza Strip (Dugan 2009). The difference is that the politics no longer fits the framework set by the establishment; no established political party is set up to capture the outrage, or the enthusiasm.

Other things are changing, including attitudes to drink. Traditionally, western HE has been lubricated if not saturated by alcohol. This part of *Brideshead Revisited* was well observed. And it is not just about student excesses. The whole image of the 'high table' is dominated by the donnish appetite for fine wines and spirits, while at the other end of the institutional pecking order, the former art college 'long lunch' was legendary. Booze also fuels the campus novel and its derivatives (see Digression 2, below).

The conditions of global HE at the beginning of the twenty-first century challenge this tradition frontally. The desire for an Islamic-friendly post-Enlightenment HE is not only domestic to the UK, but with the added value of the English-language medium, provides an international marketing opportunity. And HEIs are beginning to respond: through student unions; through campus codes; and through policies on cultural and recreational services and events. Even drink is under question (Koole 2008).

These new circumstances raise two highly sensitive questions: the first is about the concept of 'citizenship' (and how far it is a proper concern of universities); and the second is about 'extremism on campus' (and how to deal with it).

On the first, the international campus possibly leads the way in redefining the 'civic', and citizenship in particular. As John Ahier and his collaborators have shown, in a study of two very different universities (Cambridge and what is now Anglia Ruskin), contemporary students are redefining mutuality (Ahier *et al.* 2002: 141):

> In their speech, our respondents recognised four circuits: (i) those of student peers; (ii) the intergenerational; (iii) that of imagined 'abstract others' as recipients of state welfare; (iv) and the formal constitutional dimension of their relationship to state and government. These circuits were governed by principles such as fairness, altruism, reciprocity and responsibility that we will sum up in the more general term, 'mutuality' ... The moralising of extended relationships in this manner counters both the fears of those who believe that the absence of a language of formal citizenship indicates privatised withdrawal and

those who would wish to celebrate the primacy of calculative individualism.

Other scholars have shown how this process begins early (Banajai 2008).

My case is that citizenship education, certainly at the HE level and quite possibly in schools (although I declare that I know much less about this) has got it wrong. A brittle, nationalistic, quite possibly politically colonized view of what it is to understand and project rights and responsibilities as a member of a democratic and inclusive society is unpersuasive to many of that society's members (particularly youth and minorities of various kinds), and has been allowed to disguise a much more generous, contemporary sense of what it is to be a citizen. The scholarly literature points to several dangers: a perennial 'deficit' model (especially where young people are concerned); a rhetorical trend that moves very quickly and uncritically from rights to duties; a presumption that obedience and patriotism are inviolable; and a consequent ceding of the case for change to extreme groups of both the right and the left. Shakuntala Banajai's summary is devastating;

> Overwhelmingly in the global literature aimed at teaching young people and children civic values, there is an emphasis on conformity rather than critique, confrontation or challenge; in the UK, there is also an emphasis on speaking and writing in particular ways that abide by the rules and norms set by a ruling elite who show little willingness to alter policies just because citizens do not agree with them. While there is certainly a need to avoid crass populism in government, what, if anything, is the point of participation that is never going to achieve anything? At some level, civic participation and engagement begin to look like instrumental justifications for citizenship of a particular country – somewhat like a licence fee – rather than signs of citizens' political agency, maturity or power.
>
> (Banajai 2008: 557; see also Younge 2009)

Universities are central, for example, to the current prime minister's conception of 'Britishness':

> The qualities of British life – the notion of civic duty binding people to one another and the sense of fair play which underpins the idea of a proper social order – come together in the ethic of public service [leading to] the great British public institutions

admired throughout the world [among them] our universities, including the Open University.

(Brown 2004: 9)

The *summum* of this point of view is probably the 'Life in the UK' test, now mandatory for British citizenship and settlement, and memorably described by Sir Roy Strong (on GMTV on 21 January 2009) as a 'quick romp around New Labour Britain'. The test itself requires boning up on a highly specific history of immigration as well as details from the census, knowledge of a long string of 'national' and religious dates (like 'Mother's day'), knowledge about quangos, political processes (like 'what are the roles of whips?'), constitutional matters such as the Act of Succession, the composition and role of the European Union (EU), Commonwealth and United Nations (UN), as well as how to behave on the motorway, in estate agents, post offices and pubs. Some of the official practice questions are so absurd as to defy satire ('Where are children taught Welsh in schools? –A. England, B. Wales, C. Scotland, D. Northern Ireland'). Others are deeply value-laden ('What are two key features of the Civil Service? – A. Political neutrality, B. Professionalism, C. Business Knowledge, D. Party loyalty') (Dillon *et al.* 2007: 19, 29).

The TV show *Mock the Week* has a round in which contestants suggest 'additional questions for the citizenship test'. Many are right on the mark (Phillips *et al.* 2008: 64, 92):

- What is the wrong sort of snow?
- Which of the Queen's children have not been divorced?
- Can you speak a foreign language (a positive answer may not help your case)?

More seriously, history can provide a fatal critique of the official approach: '"Britishness", as the common culture of a group of human beings providing social and political leadership, has ceased to be tangible since the gentleman class abdicated. Victorian bourgeois ethics repackaged as "British values" are too vapid to be a substitute' (Acheson 2007).

In January 2009, Gordon Brown was forced to abandon his plans for a £150 million 'Museum of British History' (Tait 2009). He could be said just not to 'get' what the Muslim columnist Noorjehan Barmania (2009) described as why she (a South African) wanted to become British:

More than anything else, I wanted to become British because Britain has allowed me to flourish. It has been kind to me: in work, writing and love. And I like the British. I like the distance of their humour, their cringingly painful politeness, the innate sense of fairness, and the room for never-ending debate that allows me to be publicly critical of Britain in the first place.

I call the alternative conception 'soft citizenship' and I suggest that universities are its natural seedbed. The potential link to other forms of currently approved 'softness' (like 'soft skills', 'soft power' – and even 'female' characteristics of leadership) is deliberate. Hugh Starkey's alternative is 'cosmopolitan citizenship'. His goal is constructively to incorporate the experiences of minorities and migrants, by promoting a UN perspective based on commitments to human rights:

> Practising cosmopolitan citizenship starts with the realisation that decisions about lifestyle and personal identities are profoundly political. Certain lifestyle choices, around clothing, religious observance or leisure, for example, may bring conflict with family members, schools or the wider community. Life politics may well require involvement with the emancipatory politics associated with struggles for equal life chances.
>
> (Osler and Starkey 2005: 115)

Turning to 'struggle' and the fear that it will morph into 'extremism', Lynne Davies has explored the pedagogy of the question in the school sector in particular (Davies 2008). She draws on Sigal Bel-Porath's concept of 'belligerent nationalism' in which 'true citizens' show the qualities of courage, loyalty, responsibility, gratitude to forebears and a self-sacrificing devotion to the common good. The trouble is that in achieving this state they may be foregoing, or even evading, the critical faculties which education is established to inculcate (Davies 2008: 23, 170).

In HE, opinion is divided about both the nature and the extent of this problem. A recent study from Cambridge (Edmunds 2008) found young Muslim students 'better integrated into British society than their parents, with a stronger sense of national identity': 'contact with social democracy, multiculturalism and new generational experiences and opportunities have created a momentum for accommodation rather than a clash'. This directly contradicts the periodic warnings from Anthony Glees of the University of Buckingham's Centre for Security and Intelligence Studies that universities and colleges can be 'hotbeds of Islamic radicalism' (Lipsett 2008).

Most importantly, universities should be places where conflicts can be argued rather than fought out. A moving, if somewhat romanticized, memoir by the reformed radical Ed Husain points to his life-changing experience at the then University of North London:

> I loved my time at university. My understanding of my subject had hitherto been blinkered by the arguments of Mawdudi, Qutb and Nabhani that history was a conflict between Islam and the rest of the world. But I was determined to open up my worldview and slowly, independently, question some of the concepts and tenets I had once held dear ... Another of my tutors was Professor John Tosh, author of *The Pursuit of History*. His lectures caused me to question my approach to history. One thing history was not was an idle intellectual pastime. Professor Tosh argued that the past created the present, and that the past was open to multiple interpretations. What seemed like blasphemy at first slowly began to make sense.
>
> (Husain 2007: 156–7, 159)

Student satisfaction: complaining and appealing

Having spent generations speaking on behalf of students, universities have decided (in some cases under pressure) to ask them what they really think. There is currently an efflorescence of surveys, at the sectoral level (like the NSS – see Table 3.1), by universities generically as well as through courses, by researchers (such as the HEPI) and by commercial partners (like the student housing company UNITE). The big story here is of relatively high levels of overall satisfaction. However, these mask serious differences between subjects (much more than between institutions – to the frustration of politicians and the media) and pockets of serious unhappiness (including among some international students – see below). The high aggregate results may not, however, be secure for long. There is some evidence to support the hypothesis of a reverse Hawthorne effect: the more students are encouraged to assert their 'consumer rights', the more inclined they will be to be grumpy. Paul Ramsden, chief executive of the Higher Education Academy (HEA) said as much in his submission to the 'review' of HE commissioned by the Department for Innovation, Universities and Science (DIUS) in 2008, when talking about 'the risk of creating a self-fulfilling prophecy that today's students are more demanding consumers in relation to the quality of teaching' (he also identifies the dangers of 'survey fatigue') (Ramsden 2008, 1.7, 2.25). The 'student juries' set up by the government in 2007–8 elicited complaints about contact time, about class size, about the lack of 'guaranteed levels of service', about the lack of cost

Table 3.1 2007 and 2008 NSS results for students in England: 'I am satisfied with … '

Questions		2007	2008
		% average agreement	
1–4	The teaching on my course	82	83
5–9	Assessment and feedback	62	64
10–12	Academic support	71	73
13–15	Organization and management	71	73
16–18	Learning resources	80	81
19–21	Personal development	77	78
22	Overall satisfaction	81	82

The figures in the table are for students registered at HEIs in England. This does not include results for students at FE colleges.

Source: www.hefce.ac.uk/news/hefce/2008/nss.htm (accessed 12 September 2008, reported in Ramsden 2008).

differentiation between different subjects seen as more or less re-source intensive, and so on (BBC News Online 2008b). Perhaps particularly worrying is the evidence of a differential impact on international students identified by the HEPI student workload survey (set out in Figure 3.1) (Bekhradnia *et al.* 2006).

The question of 'what students get' by way of teaching contact and supervision – including in different types of institution – is moving up the scale of attention. HEPI was savagely criticized for showing not only radical differences between subjects but also between universities, especially because a contemporaneous European survey also seemed to suggest that that not only were UK courses shorter, but also students spent significantly less time per week on them. The HEPI data also echoes American concerns about the amount of teaching delivered by 'assistants' of various kinds in elite institutions (countered, of course, by the argument that these are the institutions with the most postgraduate researchers; that their supervisors should have minimum distraction from their own research; and in any case we are thereby developing the teachers of the future). Meanwhile, Universities UK (UUK) has allied the issue to a bid for resources, returning to 1970s-style rhetoric about the declining student:staff ratio (SSR) (Crossick 2009). (In 1973 Shirley Williams faced an outcry when she suggested that the system could operate at 13:1.) The goal

Figure 3.1   Reasons why experience was worse, or worse in some ways, by nationality (2006)

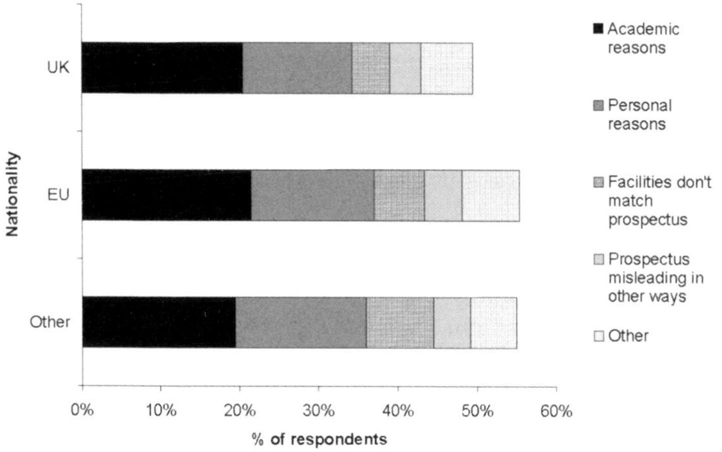

Source: Bekhradnia *et al.*(2006: 12).

is not only to garner resources, but also to preserve 'intimacy': 'The critical distinctive feature of UK higher education is the personal interaction (what has been called the intimate relationship) between students and academic staff who are acknowledged experts in their field' (FSSG 2008: 2).

A popular question is how far students now see themselves as 'customers'. In particular, higher student fees have sprung a fairly intense 'value for money' debate. Some institutions have reacted to 'consumerism' by seeking to put their relationship with the student on a 'contractual' basis, specifying what each party (the institution and the student) should undertake to provide. A survey by UUK in February 2007 (to which 70 member institutions responded) found that '13% of Universities had a formalised student contract in place, 6% were currently developing one and a further 19% were considering developing one'. Of the remaining 62 per cent none were considering following suit (McMullen 2007). Reactions have been interesting. Students, for example, have seen early attempts as distinctly one-sided.

On the wider question of contracts, virtually all UK undergraduate prospectuses contain a disclaimer that nothing in them could be deemed a contract. This opens up interesting questions about 'truth in advertising', 'trades descriptions' and prospectuses. The contract –

'implied' or not – has been tested in the UK in some celebrated cases, of which two stand out.

- In 2002, Rycotewood College in Oxfordshire was found to have breached its contract in terms of a Higher National Diploma (HND) course in historical motor vehicle restoration and conservation. The 'county court judge held that the practical content of the course was poor and that none of the teaching staff had practical experience as professional old car restorers'. The students were awarded £10,000 in damages each, including £2,500 for 'mental distress' (McMullen 2007: 2–3).
- In 2005 Oxford Brookes University was found by the Office of the Independent Adjudicator (OIA) to have misled students enrolling on an osteopathy course about the professional accreditation of the course. Although this was achieved from the General Osteopathic Society in 2005, it was not backdated for the first two cohorts entering the degree. Again compensation was paid (Ford 2005).

In most cases, HEIs will do all in their power to prevent a formal legal test of their obligations. This has led to an interesting cat-and-mouse game with the press as the latter make use of the Freedom of Information Act (Baty and Wainwright 2005).

This whole discussion confirms the obvious fact that students do not leave their legal rights at the door. David Palfreyman, bursar of New College Oxford and director of the Oxford Centre for Higher Education Policy Studies (OxCHEPS) maintains a watching brief for all developments emanating from the law of HE (Farrington and Palfreyman 2006 – see also the *Law of Higher Education: Online Casebook* at http://oxcheps.new.ox.ac.uk/new/casebook/). While noting due judicial deference to expert academic judgement in areas like admissions, teaching and assessment – albeit not if exercised in an arbitrary or capricious way (see the discussion of the differences between complaining and appealing below) – he stresses the applicability of aspects of contract law, of tort (or 'civil wrong') in relation to negligence or malpractice, or landlord and tenant law in relation to residences, and of public law and judicial review.

There is also the more general question of a duty of care. In the *THE* of 3 July 2008, the University of Salford advertised for a 'head of student wellbeing'. The 'motivated, ambitious individual' in question should have 'experience of managing teams who proactively support diversity and enable student wellbeing ... knowledge of disability support systems and an understanding of mental health issues', as well as the ability 'to contribute to a package of support for our growing number of international students'.

Approaches like this reflect a growing realization that as participation in UK HE has grown, and as traditional 'screening mechanisms' have fallen away (admissions were never simply about academic achievement or potential in the ways that opponents of expansion claim), the student community is going to look a lot more like the community at large. This will include the presentation of problems, such as mental health.

Complaining and appealing are, of course, two different things. The former is in the zone of consumer satisfaction: 'this service isn't what I expected, what I deserve, or what you said it would be'. The latter is in the territory of judgement: 'you got it wrong when you assessed me, dismissed me, or determined my fate in some other way'. In both arenas questions of substance and process can become entangled with each other. In some senses the resulting dilemmas are similar to those experienced in all large, complex organizations in the modern world. However, there is one way in which the crossover can prove especially toxic for the HE community. That is when errors of process can create questions about the quality of academic judgement and its effects on progress and awards.

This is a tightrope walked by the OIA, established following the Higher Education Act of 2004. In its third annual report, covering the calendar year 2007, the OIA noted a rise in applications (up by 25 per cent from 586 in 2006 to 734), a slight rise in the number upheld 'to some extent' (to 26 per cent), a higher proportion (than their representation in the student body) of complaints from postgraduates (36 per cent), from older students (25 per cent over 25) and from students in subjects allied to medicine (where there are special issues about retaining student status while the complaint is heard). There may be some understandable reason for the heavy trade in complaints from mature students on vocational courses: not only do they have a lot invested, but there is also the complication of judgements about 'fitness' or 'licence' to practise. Overall, two-thirds of complaints were about academic results, and 11 per cent about disciplinary matters including plagiarism (OIA 2008).

Digression 2: falling in (and out of) love

What constitutes professional behaviour by staff of all types, and what can be the legitimate expectations of staff by students, lies behind many of these controversies. What happens, however, when the relationship moves beyond the professional? What happens when love fades and is replaced by power, including the power of the weak over the strong?

Sex and power have, of course, been the staples of the campus novel, as brilliantly dissected by Elaine Showalter (2005). And the story goes on. Some of my favourite examples are not included by Showalter. Sometimes the treatment in these is picaresque, as in the apparently deserved torture of Sydney Pyke, a professor of media studies, by a combination of arch feminists and jet-setting students in David Caute's *The Women's Hour* (1993). Sometimes it is unashamedly bawdy, as in the campaign by his delicious fianceé to shock the hero of Joseph Heller's *Good as Gold*: 'I'm a Sarah Lawrence girl, even though I didn't finish there, and they always told me to speak the truth as I saw it. At Bennington, you know, we had this professor of art we used to keep score with. Three hundred and twenty of us fucked him in the two years he was there' (Heller 1979: 408).

Sometimes it is radically alternative, as in Robert Littell's post-war fantasy, *The Visiting Professor* (1993). Sometimes it represents just humdrum blackmail, as in David Lodge's *Deaf Sentence*, or the anonymous story of *A Campus Conspiracy* (Anonymous 2006; Lodge 2008). If anything, the balance of predation in the literature is of students chasing teachers (I suspect in the real world the opposite is true). However, many cases are deeply ambiguous: ambiguity perhaps reaching its height in David Mamet's 1992 play, *Oleana*. In it the teacher (John) has all of the power vested in his office, but it is the student (Carol) who prevails, as his tenure is apparently denied on the grounds of her complaint (Mamet 1992: 64, 68–9). Neither wins.

Culturally, British HE has always been more tolerant than North American institutions about staff/student sexual relations. Various spokespersons are more inclined to say things such as the following: 'we can't help it' (Alan Ryan – former warden of New College, Oxford); 'the teaching/learning relationship ought not to lose its erotic force' (Mary Beard – professor of classics at Cambridge); 'arrangements like blind and double marking prevent abuse, it's not like doctors and their patients, or therapists and their clients' (Michael Reiss – professor of science education at the Institute of Education, University of London); and (in celebrated cases) 'look at the matches that have been made'. The UK unions are on the fence: the Universities and Colleges Union (UCU) is quoted as follows:

'while staff are strongly advised to declare such relationships, failure to disclose should not, in itself constitute grounds for disciplinary action' (all quotations from Fearn 2008b).

I think this represents a collective cop-out. The data is just too strong on what happens when judgement is undermined or affection fades. In these circumstances, simple 'declaration' will not be enough, not only for the happy couple, but also for their peers. After all, the teaching relationship has a defined end-point; the personal tie can await consummation until then. Whatever happened to deferred gratification, of which the case of Billy Crystal's schoolboy character and his teacher in the ground-breaking soap opera *Soap* ought to be the defining case? They managed to keep their hands off each other – to great comic effect – until he graduated.

If there is a message in this chapter as a whole, it is probably that institutions and their representatives can afford to trust students more. In general, students – at all levels – have rational and legitimate expectations of 'their' HE. In general they understand the 'deal' that goes with achieving these expectations. They should expect a caring as well as a challenging study environment; but they have the same rights as any other member of the community to pursue happiness, including through unhappiness.

4

UNHAPPY STAFF

Staff members occupy a significantly different force-field from students. Are they primarily, employees, creators of the university agenda, or guardians of values under threat? What are the implications of the answers to these questions for their rights, responsibilities and morale? In particular, how have the relationships between the different professional groups contributing to the HE enterprise changed as a result?

The staff estate

The HE workforce covers an extraordinary range of professional and support operations. In many ways each institution is an entire society on its own (the ex-Canberra VC Don Aitken once likened his to a turbulent Italian Renaissance town) (Watson 2000: 85). Meanwhile, this microcosm lives in a series of alternative macrocosms: its host society; the rest of the HE business; and an increasingly interdependent global sector.

The effects on staff pull in different directions. To take retention and mobility first: a study of the UK sector undertaken in September 2006 by the firm i-graduate with the *THES* revealed simultaneous stasis and restlessness. Just under half of university staff planned to leave their current jobs within two years. Around a quarter, who had been in one institution for more than five years, planned to stay indefinitely (i-graduate 2006).

Like students, as the HE system grows, staff are beginning to look more like the society as a whole, but – as set out below – more slowly. UK HE is also big business, with 300,000 employees in 2006–7.

The UK system is becoming more international (non-UK national employees grew from 4,000 to 11,000 between 1996 and 2007) and more ethnically diverse (in 2006–7 6 per cent were from ethnic minorities and 16 per cent from overseas). Gender equality is arriving more slowly, and is taking a long time to penetrate the higher levels: almost 50 per cent of teaching staff are female (having increased from 48 per cent between 1996 and 2007), but only 20 per cent of professors are women. Only one VC is from an ethnic minority in 2009. Subject mix counts – again as for students: 60 per cent of education staff are female; but only 14 per cent are in engineering (Data from HEFCE 2009: Ch. 2). What this data means is that, if the student body is moving fast to reflect the composition of the wider society, it is taking the staff profile some time to catch up. Only 26 per cent of academic staff are aged under 35, and 20 per cent are 55 or over (although the average age is dropping fast – it is currently 42.7). Only 2 per cent declare a disability (UUK 2008).

People are organized in different ways inside universities and colleges. In ironic contrast to the 'flatness' discussed in Chapter 6, most participants would imagine a hierarchy, something like the following:

- senior management;
- 'academic' (teaching) staff (or 'faculty');
- 'professional' support staff;
- contract researchers;
- clerical staff;
- manual 'workers'.

In the UK there are, I think, enduring differences between those institutions founded by royal charter and those created by Act of Parliament (the so-called 'statutory' universities) in this respect: the former had the legacy of a strict demarcation between 'faculty' and 'administration' (often enshrined in institutional charters and statues); employees in the latter were all 'public sector HE' workers originally responsible to the local authority personnel department. Celia Whitchurch has explored this legacy, and its continued impact on relationships between different categories of staff in different types of institution (Whitchurch 2008a). Another divergence is in the ways in which individuals have built their careers and developed esteem among their peers. In the 'chartered' sector, research ruled (although perhaps not to quite the extent that some have claimed – as in president of the Royal Society Lord Robert May's constant re-iteration that the Research Assessment Exercise [RAE] has become 'the only game in town'). In the 'public' sector, curriculum development and in particular (large) course leadership was a path to recognition and reward. The 'merged' system has, of course, tilted towards the former.

There are also stories from some 'hybrids' who fit in awkwardly. Again Celia Whitchurch is a valuable guide to the new species of 'niche builders', 'project-workers' and 'pathfinders' (Whitchurch 2009; see also Bacon 2009).

The 'university hierarchy' is strongly reminiscent of Jim Bouton's description of a major league baseball club in *Ball Four* – one of the New York Public Library's books of the last century. The book is about the author's personal and professional tribulations as a former top pitcher trying to re-establish himself in the top flight after injury. Bouton's professional baseball club hierarchy goes something like this:

- owner;
- star player (sometimes called 'the franchise');
- manager;
- established players;
- coaches;
- marginal players (Bouton 1970).

The story is, in effect, about his fall from somewhere between Levels 2 and 3 to Level 6 of this pecking order. Taking the bottom three levels from Bouton (which is where most of his story takes place, with both established players and coaches exercising their authority over the marginal players, like Bouton), think about the analogy with the short-term contract researcher: who pushes him or her around, how and why?

Nonetheless, the university or college does exist as an entity for some purposes and in some contexts, especially when viewed from outside. What it is seen as doing to or for a client is seen usually as a *corporate* responsibility (you have only to experience a VC's postbag to understand this – see Chapter 6, Digression 8). Incidentally, one of the things that, in my experience, most infuriates senior managers is when quite senior members of the organization say 'why doesn't the university do something about x?' as if they have nothing to do with it.

More seriously, if the reification of the university is to have positive effects, it is normally the management who have to take some responsibility for defining and reflecting it, even if they do so by stealth. On stealth, the classic formulation is Eric Ashby's in *Technology and the Academics* (1958), about seeding your best ideas with others, and nodding approvingly when they come back under different ownership. Graeme Davies, VC of London, has recently said almost exactly the same thing: 'there is no limit to what you can achieve provided that you are prepared to take no credit for it' (private communication). Meanwhile, in his essay of Maoist self-criticism, *Excellence Without a Soul*, Henry Lewis, longstanding dean of Harvard College, declares 'there is no upstairs and downstairs in a healthy college':

> Students talk all the time to the police officers, the medical trainers, the financial aid officers, not to mention those with official advising and counselling roles. The employees at the bottom of the organizational tree are the ones who see students the most. They too are educators. They absorb the spirit of the institution and convey its values to students every day.
>
> (Lewis 2007: 256–7)

However, there is a downside to Lewis' description of moral 'flatness' in the university, as shown in this story from Australia (the author, Sharon Bell, was then the deputy VC of Canberra, writing about a friend who lasted less than a year as dean of humanities at the University of Melbourne). Both the author and her subject are now in different institutions:

> Being a dean in an arts faculty is very tough. Why? Because colleagues in the social sciences and humanities have been trained to be hyper-critical. Their disciplinary expertise provides them with a toolbox of devices to dissect and unravel the implementation of the best-intended strategic initiatives. They increasingly exercise this talent in extraordinarily difficult funding environments ... They operate in an environment in which a quickly written email may generate detailed semiotic analysis and imputation of ill intent.
>
> In the academic environment, very clever people may turn their very clever minds to negative ends. We can understand and rationalise this. It reflects in some ways colleagues' passionate commitment to their discipline, to their scholarship and their intellectual autonomy. It reflects the influence of the challenging, under-resourced environment in which we work.
>
> But it also may reflect an unwillingness to exercise what John Paul Lederach calls the moral imagination, the ability to empathise, to build peace, in this case with those who do their best to lead.
>
> (Bell 2007)

David Sims (2005) has examined this process of 'demonization' (as well as the 'joy of denunciation') in great detail. It can involve powerful emotions like anger, but also joy and guilt. As a result, 'bullying' has a particular resonance in an academic culture, where the expectation of challenge to established authority is a notable design feature. There are, however, especially vulnerable groups: contract researchers, part-time teachers, and clerical and support workers (see the discussion of hierarchies above). Loraleigh Keashley and Joel Neuman of the State University of New York (SUNY) at New Paltz have created a 'Workplace Aggression Research Questionnaire' which has been used by several American institutions to study themselves. The questionnaire asks individuals, for example, whether 'they have been glared at, yelled at, or subjected to mean pranks over the past six months' (Fogg 2008). Darla Twale and Barbara De Luca have meanwhile proposed that the overall culture of academe 'has all the right ingredients to make it [bullying] grow' (Twale and De Luca 2008, quoted in Fogg 2008).

However, as Bell's narrative indicates, the story may be more complicated than many of the 'fix the managers' school wish to concede. Academic culture can be home to a special type of lateral, or 'upwards' 'ganging up' that does it no credit. This problem is acknowledged in the Chartered Management Institute (CMI) annual surveys of 'bullying at work' where it is noted that across the range of respondents: 'bullying does not occur exclusively in formal hierarchical relationships between managers and their line reports, although this is the most commonly-observed relationship ... bullying is also reported as occurring between peers, subordinates, line managers and external customers or clients' (CMI 2008: 3.6).

This is not to say that everybody is unhappy. Here is Andrew Oswald (2007), scourge of the QAA (and of university management in general), and joint inventor of the Oswald-Zizzo effect (which finds that we would be prepared to reduce our incomes in order that others – notably the 'less deserving' – should also suffer):

For the first time in 20 years, I advise you to pursue a career in universities. It has been a long slog through decades of red-tape and low-wage mediocrity, but British academic jobs are finally attractive ... In the world of scholarship, one encounters an extraordinary dedication to ideas and a generosity of intellectual spirit. I still find that marvellous.

It is a central empirical thesis of this book that working in HE is at the same time hugely frustrating and immensely satisfying. It may be one of these things almost all of the time for some staff members. Others may flip between the two states at an alarming rate.

Pay and security may play a key role here, as set out in the longitudinal research of Gail Kinman and Fiona Jones, whose main conclusions are that 'UK academics are highly committed but are likely to experience low job satisfaction and poor health because their efforts are not recognised with job security and a fair salary' (Kinman and Jones 2008). The juxtaposition of the late 2008 economic downturn, and the final phase of a two-year settlement for UK university staff (that was pegged to inflation in September 2008 – at 5 per cent – just before it dived) may cause some attitudes to be revised. Certainly the Universities and Colleges Employers' Association (UCEA) jumped in quickly with a news release (dated 14 November) based on the government's Annual Survey of Hours and Earnings (ASHE) to claim that a 'higher education academic's pay is significantly more than other professionals'. Above all, academia may offer one of the best validations of what should be called (Friedrich) Herzberg's theorem (it has also proved strongly resistant to performance-related pay). As interpreted by Simon Caulkin of *The Observer* (2009a): 'Investigating motivation at work, he [Herzberg] concluded that although pay and conditions could cause *dis*satisfaction, the reverse was not true: they didn't generate satisfaction, which comes from factors intrinsic to the job itself (challenging work, recognition, responsibility)'.

The role of unions and professional associations is also relevant. UK universities are relatively weakly unionized on the academic side of the house; a merger between two 'inherited' binary groups (the National Association of Teachers in Further and Higher Education [NATFHE] and the Association of University Teachers [AUT] into the Universities and Colleges Union [UCU]) having, if anything, resulted in an organization weaker than the sum of its parts. Meanwhile on the support side, UNISON (the 'public service union') has played a cannier and arguably more effective hand. The employers have had their own problems of discipline and strategy, as reflected in the somewhat tortured history of the UCEA. They have, however, succeeded in the goal of negotiating and then driving through a single 'framework' agreement, which has more or less stuck across the sector (and kept a somewhat attenuated version of national bargaining extant) (UCEA 2008). Neither side has even begun to contemplate the response to the credit crunch in the USA, which is seeing voluntary pay cuts, 'furloughs' (periods of mandatory unpaid leave) and both voluntary and involuntary lay-offs (the term of art is 'retrenchment') across the full spectrum of institutions.

On higher ground, western university staff members have – like the students – lost the apparent romantic flavour of their now not so recent past. The heroic campaigns have been around academic freedom, including that of members of other systems (like the many refugees assisted by the AUT to re-establish their careers away from Nazi Germany). The less appealing campaigns have been in the classic arena of unionism: pay and conditions (including pensions), and what has become known as 'casualization' (the movement of full-time into part-time posts). In the UK, hotspots like redundancies, subject or departmental closures, can spark local and wider protest, as do occasional individual cases (following disciplinary or other action).

A tale of two surveys ∎

The year 2007 was the tenth anniversary of the Dearing Report, which included the last serious attempt to ask the sector as a whole what it thought. To set a context for the deliberations of the main Committee, a survey was commissioned, as a result of which some 805 responses and around 6,000 pages of text were analysed by a team led by Ron Barnett of the Institute of Education and published as the Inquiry's background *Report I*. Despite the air of crisis that surrounded the Committee's work, the tone was fundamentally positive and optimistic (see NCIHE 1997: 3–8).

In a book to mark the anniversary, launched at a conference in July 2007, Michael Amoah and I attempted a modest re-run of a sector-wide survey of opinions about the state of the HE nation. We asked 100 selected individuals what they thought about the experience of the last 10 years (numbers below refer to the individual respondents; other than those identified as 'anonymous' all were prepared to 'sign' their work, although none are named in what follows).

Here are three of the voices reported in *The Dearing Report: Ten Years On* (Watson and Amoah 2007). The contrast between the first two and the third is stark.

- 'I genuinely believe that this is the most exciting time in HE that I have known in 30 years in the profession' (35 – Russell Group pro-vice-chancellor [PVC]).
- 'I am frustratingly satisfied with my role over the last 10 years in HE administration' (54 – Russell Group assistant registrar).
- 'Despite universities achieving overall excellent teaching and research results over the last decade they are in general pretty unhappy places. The sheer number of students in large institutions means they feel like, and are often treated like, just numbers. The

main aim of the next 10 years should be to make universities happy places to work and study. While this might seem a very basic point, if we wish people to have lifelong engagement with universities they must feel at home in them and also the costs associated with unhappy staff and students can be enormous' (60 – principal lecturer, 'new' university).

Table 4.1 identifies the 100 voices, broken down by role, characteristics and years of service. Basically the consensus was positive when reviewing the past ten years: 57 per cent considered that 'the UK system is improving in teaching' (9 per cent strongly); 61 per cent thought the same about research (16 per cent strongly); 63 per cent about services to business (11 per cent strongly); and 50 per cent about service to society (11 per cent strongly).

Turning to their own institutions, 57 per cent saw improvement in teaching (14 per cent strongly); 48 per cent in research (29 per cent

Table 4.1   The 100 voices

Roles (%)

Heads of institutions (3)
Deputies or PVCs (13)
Senior administrators (21)
Other administrators (24)
HE 'experts' (20) (scholars in the field as well as those professionally involved in analysing its progress)
HE 'agencies' (9)
Professional bodies (including unions) (5)
Academics under 40 (5)
Student leaders (1)

Characteristics (%)
Male (58)
Female (42)

'Academic' (46)
'Support' (54)

Years of service (%)
1–10 (22)
11–20 (43)
21–30 (22)
31–40 (14)

Source: Watson and Amoah (2007: 110–11)

strongly); 53 per cent in services to business (18 per cent strongly); and 53 per cent in service to society (13 per cent strongly). The juxtaposition with views of the system as a whole (above) is interesting, with the implication that teaching is about the same, but that the collective performance in other areas – especially research – is stronger.

However, there were some questions about which they were seriously divided. For example, 27 per cent thought that 'student motivation has declined in the last 10 years' (2 per cent strongly), contrasted with 33 per cent who thought that 'student performance has improved in the past 10 years' (2 per cent felt this strongly but 40 per cent were unsure or saw little change). Some 58 per cent found institutions to be 'well-managed on the whole' (6 per cent strongly) and 64 per cent felt that 'the sector is still significant' (23 per cent strongly), but the question of whether funding should be increased from private sources split as follows: yes 40 per cent, no 51 per cent. On the question of whether or not 'public confidence in HE has declined over the past 10 years' the split was: yes 33 per cent, no 34 per cent, undecided 32 per cent and one 'spoilt' vote. Similarly (with more indecision) the proposition that UK HE 'is winning a global race' split: yes 22 per cent, no 25 per cent, undecided 44 per cent.

In their open-ended responses, the 100 voices converged on a number of propositions (the respondents' punctuation, spelling and emphasis has been retained in all direct quotations below).

The first was that HE is a satisfying place to be, especially because of self-management:

> I get enormous satisfaction from my job but believe I am very lucky. The university appreciates my skills and plays to my strengths – I have enormous autonomy and am not bogged down by administration. So I can get on with doing research and trying to influence policy development. I still do some teaching (but only about 3 hours a week) and enjoy that contact and challenge.
>
> (5 – 'new' university professor)

> I appreciate the responsibility and the relative luxury of being able to manage my own work and that my ideas are valued, even if they aren't always acted on. Dissatisfaction comes from having too much to do and not enough time to plan.
>
> (21 – manager in a Russell Group business school)

> As an academic, the main satisfaction lay in very great freedom over how to spend my time, coupled with a reliable income. A

combination not open to many – and one which remained true
even though the pressures on time grew over the years.

(27 – chief executive of a funding council)

As DVC [deputy vice-chancellor], I am responsible for the scope,
management and quality of the Academic Programme [learning
and research]. It is a great privilege to be in such a role, as I feel
passionately that civil society and a sound economy need excellent higher education, in which students can begin to realise
their full potential, and in which high quality research generates
knowledge for society and the economy. I derive great satisfaction from new programmes being approved, new inter-
disciplinary initiatives in research and learning being
established, from the buzz of what the students are saying in and
around the campus, from colleagues' delight when books and
papers are published, research grants won. I am surprised by the
conservatism of some colleagues, some of whom embrace innovation and new ideas with much less enthusiasm than I expected, and tend to focus on small issues rather than the big
picture of what we are trying to achieve.

(51 – DVC at an 'old' university)

I consider it an honour and a privilege to be a VC. Enormous
satisfaction from setting the tone and strategic direction of the
University.

(55 – anonymous VC)

Having now retired from a long career in HE, I can reflect clearly
on what gave me most satisfaction – it was the joy of seeing a
student able to use the understanding I had given him/her to
solve a problem, and in particular, to design a product or system
to satisfy a real need. This tangible outcome is what makes engineering so satisfying.

(74 – professor emeritus, 'new' university)

Whilst the challenges seem to increase each year, the satisfaction
of working in an intellectually stimulating environment out-
weigh these, even for those in non-academic roles. There is still a
sense of higher education as a force for personal development
and social good despite the potential dangers of the reductive
skills-led approach of the current policy agenda.

(79 – head of registry, 'old' university)

Perhaps naturally, such enthusiasm was sometimes considerably qualified:

> The great attraction of higher education remains the control one has over one's intellectual life. Dissatisfaction concerns especially the tension between teaching (and being a conscientious colleague) and research that has been exacerbated in favour of the latter this past two decades. Teaching is important, but there are few career rewards here; accordingly, we now have much teaching time sacrificed to research that has little value to students, but is the royal route to promotion.
>
> (29 – anonymous professor)

> My role is not typical. I have a temporary role working on University projects. I found it satisfying to write generic role profiles for academic staff from part-time lecturer to professor/head of department. This allowed me to think about the University's expectations of academic staff in an environment where teaching, course-related administration and the occasional research article just isn't enough. I found it satisfying to undertake a review of learning and teaching, to consider the reasons why the University does not have a better L&T profile and to make recommendations for change. I do, though, feel strongly dissatisfied. I am not a decision-maker, I do not line manage or work closely with academic staff, I am not involved in curriculum development and I have hardly any contact with students.
>
> (52 – project manager in a 'new' university)

The most regular, and most forcefully expressed, complaint was that the government needs to match its rhetoric with investment:

> Government should invest in UK HE if it is to continue to compete successfully internationally – among other things, this will help ensure recruitment of overseas students against strong global competition.
>
> (16 – conservatoire assistant director)

> The government should invest properly in HE and education generally. I would also like to see the government's focus on skills/employability widen to also value education as 'Bildung'.
>
> (18 – research manager in a specialist institution)

> The financial pressures on teaching in particular will continue to require co-funding by the Government, graduates and

organisations that benefit from HE. Investing in higher levels of learning is vital if the UK is to be internationally competitive. Participation levels are too low and more younger and older people need the underpinning qualifications as well as aspiration to support their lifelong learning in an increasingly challenging international economic environment.

(22 – chief executive of a sector-wide body)

Government (UK and devolved) needs to take a realistic view of what can be afforded and what it will buy; and not pretend to be buying more than is being paid for. If world class is what is wanted, then, while accepting the need for the sector to be able to show that it is using money effectively, government has to fund (or enable market mechanisms) appropriately.

(27 – funding council chief executive)

Not that this is always just about levels of funding; for several it is also to do with strategy and method:

The rhetoric of flexible delivery, lifelong learning and widening participation would be made real and substantial by changes to the funding methodology (in England). Credit based funding would enable HEIs to be much more innovative in their development of CPD and other flexible programmes. The government also needs to make a substantial commitment to the Bologna process and look seriously at its implications rather than presiding over the half-hearted muddle that we currently have.

(31 – PVC of a 'new' university)

Governments should take seriously their rhetoric about success in the knowledge economy being crucial to the future health and prosperity of the nations and be prepared to make a step change in public investment to achieve this benefit.

(44 – funding council chief executive)

I still feel that UK Higher Education is relatively under-funded, despite recent government investment in research, which is to be welcomed. I would like to see government pay the full cost of teaching science subjects, and to enable institutions to afford to continue to offer languages, even when student numbers are falling. We need to be able to balance our books, respond to student demand but also have an eye to the country's strategic needs for the future: a tightrope if ever there was one! Information technology could improve the staff and student experience, and institutions' investment in it needs to be enabled and incentivised, probably by HEFCE. There needs to be a leadership programme which is affordable by the sector, as we must invest in the leadership skills of our staff and the next generation of leaders. Institutions must use their resources for this.

(51 – DVC of an 'old' university)

However, the same correspondent goes on to share the blame: 'Institutions themselves must take responsibility for ensuring continuous improvement and appropriate diversity of mission: we cannot blame the government for everything!' A similar expression of shared responsibility comes from this correspondent:

Increased investment in HE infrastructure funding (Govt.) – an urgent priority. Less planning prescription and centralised management (Govt. and HEFCE). More delegated decision-making and more incentive funding to provide a genuinely diverse HE sector (Govt., HEFCE, HEIs). A public debate and some consensus about the MODERN purpose and vision for HE on a societal and economic level – and hence some rational proposals for where the balance of funding (between public, private and the individual) should lie.

(57 – senior manager in a research-funding foundation)

Universities have achieved a lot over the last 10 years and are one of the few success stories in the UK economy – this would suggest that they do not need additional government direction, audit or control.

(68 – 'new' university VC)

Incidentally, this correspondent was one of several who demonstrated how much we live in the moment (as was also true of contributors to Dearing Report) by focusing many of his remarks on the 2007 Further Education Act (then going through Parliament).

The harshest criticism of both sides came from the chief executive of a key sector-wide body, who wished to remain anonymous: 'Government should stand back from trying to control the future of higher education and HE's vision should be more imaginative and richer than simply demanding more money and subscribing to fashionable policies'. A similar point was made forcefully by correspondent 43 (a Russell Group registrar): 'Government should try to suppress its instinct to treat universities as part of the public sector'.

Most agreed that research was vulnerable; although in the same mode as some of the 'split votes' referred to above, this was a consequence of both too much and too little selectivity:

> We are a relatively small system in global terms, and Scotland is a small sub-set of that small system. I very much doubt whether our current collective research ambitions are sustainable. The question is therefore not whether selectivity is inevitable, but what shape it will take.
>
> (1 – DVC of an 'old' university)

> I gain immense satisfaction from most aspects of working in HE – teaching students, researching in areas of interest, contributing in a collegial way to management, and having a job which is flexible and hierarchically flat. Dissatisfactions are not great, but I get frustrated at the side-effects of the Research Assessment Exercise in terms of its cyclical impact on the job market for new entrants to the profession, its forcing of academics into narrow subject areas, and its prescriptive influence on the sorts of research and writing which is rated.
>
> (13 – reader in an 'old' university)

> Designate a dozen universities as research centres; the rest to be teaching only. Take undergraduates out of the top dozen, so a different league of teaching universities might be established. Stop the RAE and campaign for teaching to be valued in higher education by promoting and rewarding good teaching. Allow only the top dozen to award doctoral degrees, the rest to teach to Masters level. (I remain anonymous in this return precisely because the risks of criticising the current research obsessions are high – my dept is anticipating lots of 3/4 scores in 2008. How can critics of the RAE expect such results? So I practice, but don't believe.)
>
> (29 – anonymous professor)

> Research is now more competitive and successful, in part due to the RAE. Changes to the RAE and the funding of research will pose questions on what research can take place if departments that are not research graded are unable to receive funding. There are also questions on academic freedom and the ability to research independently of the state while still receiving financial income from the state.
>
> (70 – senior administrator in a sector-wide research body)

If concentration of research funding divided the group, there was more agreement that in many of its practices the sector will be required to 'loosen up'. Here are three very similar predictions/ prescriptions from different parts of the sectoral forest:

> The other aspect from a Scottish perspective is the long term impact of short cycle HE delivered by non-HEI institutions. Is this the harbinger of a more general loosening up of HE delivery? Or is it to be a merely national and possibly short lived response to local contingent circumstances?
>
> (1 – 'old' university DVC)

> More resources need to be channelled into universities with high proportions of 'widening participation' type students so we can ensure these students can succeed. And less emphasis in HE policies about meeting the needs of the economy. Employers – need to change their attitudes to HE, including rewarding students who have not completed their degrees, rather than penalising them as a failure. HEIs and HEFCE – much more flexibility in provision e.g. credit framework and changes in funding mechanisms so that the divide between full and part time students is eroded and so that students really can 'stop out' rather than drop out. Introduce a national bursary scheme that all HEIs contribute towards and scrap OFFA. DfES/ESRC – fund more longitudinal studies on 14–25 year olds so we have a better understanding of participation and the impact of HE policies. Contrary to the trend, increase the length of the degree to 4 years for the most disadvantaged students.
>
> (5 – 'new' university professor)

> In my own institution (a Mixed Economy College) I welcome the emerging emphasis on widening participation and employer engagement. In a period of change, the sector needs the freedom to innovate and take properly controlled risks to ensure that new learners are engaged and new approaches tried. Providing leadership and direction in this period is a challenge but also an opportunity to play a role in re-shaping the landscape of the higher education system.
>
> (11 – FE principal)

Another strong consensus was about the need to get 'beyond instrumentalism'. Correspondent 34 (a 'new' university professor and head of academic development) spoke of the 'need to re-assert the civic purposes of the university'. Correspondent 59 (a 'new' university associate dean) echoed this sentiment: 'I would dearly love undergraduate qualifications to be broader and for postgraduate qualifications to provide the vocational focus, but I am swimming against the tide here'. The chief executive of another sector-wide body (65) linked this with our 'civilising role in society'. Here too the voices come from all across a diverse body of institutions and professional roles. Here are four examples:

> The challenge in my role is having to continually reconcile my values as an academic and an IT professional with a promoted culture that preaches education as merely an instrument. The irony is that to be a successful and effective professional, core 'liberal' HE values such as critical inquiry [are] key. My main challenge is persuading my students to engage with this.
>
> (7 – 'old' university senior lecturer)

> There needs to be a re-establishment of the worth of 'teaching'. There needs to be an emphasis on academic 'output' as well as 'input'. HE should be less comfortable for some! It should be recognised that every HEI has a right to have research ambitions, engage in research activity and be supported to do this. Although the sector needs to be aware of and responsive to the market it is important to remember that we cannot be as reactive to market conditions as the commercial sector and our customers expect more from us than market principles. Education is an 'experience' as much as a 'commodity' and the experience can often be more enriching than the qualification gained.
>
> (15 – 'new' university school manager)

> HEIs are currently in danger of losing their academic autonomy to government and employer interests, and higher education is rapidly moving towards being no more than advanced 'skills' training. This is a serious threat to the important humane values that underpin higher learning. Higher education should not have to justify itself on the grounds of short-term economic utility: it is one of the few human activities which is sufficiently justified by its continuous achievements over decades and centuries.
>
> (72 – anonymous sector body CEO)

> Universities must preserve the quality of education and the opportunity to pursue 'pure' research. They must promote the value of a 'liberal' education that develops individuals and their

ability to contribute to society, running alongside education relevant to professional and employment requirements.

(75 – Russell Group project manager)

The biggest bugbear for the 100 was the way HE is portrayed in and characterized by the media. Correspondent 57 (from the research foundation) spoke of the need for 'an accessible public debate'. Most forthright was 7 (the 'old' university senior lecturer):

I would like the British media to grow up regarding education. The education system that produced many senior journalists is wholly unsuitable for modern society. If they do not realise this then I must assume that their well-funded higher education was wasted. Government has been complicit in their inaction. If they want to mean what they say about Britain's future knowledge economy, then they need to make it clear that harking back to a mythical golden age is not a sensible option. We need a mature debate about how all levels of the UK education system can meet the desire and aspirations of its citizens and we need it now. Without this, I doubt that much else can happen.

Correspondent 19 (an 'old' university registrar) pointed again to collusion:

Public confidence has not been helped by HE's seeming willingness to allow others – notably the media – to define the terms. The most obvious example of this is league tables, where Dearing gave us the opportunity to define our own but we didn't.

This spirit of Maoist self-criticism also sparked some thoughts about those parts of the system apparently resistant to change at all costs. Our FE principal (11) referred to 'institutional protectionism' and correspondent 32 (an Oxbridge admissions officer) similarly pointed to the 'need to balance the preservation of core values and a healthy suspicion of "change for change's sake" with a willingness to adapt and develop in the interests of society as a whole – not just the academic community'. Respondent 8 (an administrator in one of the University of London's specialist centres) described 'one of the most challenging aspects of my job' as 'working with people who resist all change at all costs, even if it means blocking positive developments in the process'. The starkest critique came from a senior manager who requested anonymity:

I think there has been too long a tradition of laissez faire and slack management in some parts of higher education, which defies any sense of public accountability. In some quarters there is a real defensiveness and rush to grievance, which prevents progress. We have to be accountable to the public, and to account for our performance in this highly privileged sector. Furthermore, the many excellent colleagues who work to the limits deserve a management approach which does not accept that they will carry their less committed or well performing colleagues. I know that this is counter culture in some quarters, but we do need to be fair in our approach. That is sometimes tough in a naturally challenging sector.

Finally (in terms of the more or less consensual elements) was a suggestion that the sector needed to work hard to get up to speed with international and global issues:

The main challenges I am facing are increased competition and uncertainty in the global market for students. It has become much more difficult, for example, to accurately forecast student numbers. I also face challenges within my institution from continued scepticism in some quarters about the value of student recruitment and a reluctance to engage with the University's international strategy.

(47 – Russell Group admissions officer)

It would be great if the Universities were able to invest more in their academic interface both in terms of staffing and resources to address the global issues and the place of UK HE on the world scene. Consolidation with our European partners would be a good idea and would enable the European HE to develop more consistently as well as develop new approaches to the UK position. The UK will start to fall behind the China/Australian/Asian partnerships if there is not a real investment in HE.

(71 – academic development officer, specialist institution)

Having spent time in China, I am staggered with the speed of change there. There is truly a national sense of an educational revolution (all levels). They genuinely believe in the power of HE for change. I know many critics are sceptical here (Will Hutton, for example), due to the ideological inheritance, but when you see the Mao statues on campus coming down quietly in the night, know that all Tsinghua students are armed with a laptop on arrival, see the scale of English language teaching nationally you know this is a country on the march. What happens when most of the world's software is written in Mandarin? Will the Anglo-Saxons still be up there?

(73 – language centre manager, 'old' university)

Question 10 raises the question of the location of UK higher in a 'global race'. This is an issue which has come to the fore to an even greater extent since the publication of Dearing and raises interesting issues about the impact of globalisation on higher education. Some commentators (e.g. the work of some of the 2006 Fulbright New Century Scholars) make the case that we may be seeing the emergence of 'super universities' almost detached from their host nation states. Yet is it these exceptions which – at great economic and other expense – are acting as models for the vast majority of the whole sector?

(78 – 'new' university PVC)

As for more specific things 'to be done', eight suggestions received fairly general support. The first was more, and more specific, staff development. An 'old' university registrar (19) pointed to:

the great paradox of universities not being good at training or developing staff for current and future roles and a general reluctance to invest in people in a planned way [as well as] the persistent 'we are so different' culture which makes it difficult to open up staff attitudes to different ways of doing things.

Respondent 43 (a Russell Group registrar) similarly identified the need for 'huge strides in HR management in universities and a significant improvement in leadership and development'.

Respondent 17 (a Russell Group PVC) suggested:

Improve the quality and training of everybody involved in the teaching of students. I have always favoured a compulsory mechanism to ensure that our staff are helped to develop their teaching skills for the benefit of students.

The second suggestion was about continuing to press on the difficult issue of employer engagement. The sector-wide chief executive (22) most involved in the area stressed this as a top priority:

There remain challenges to help both higher education and businesses better define their respective boundaries and roles. It is NOT the role of HE to produce 'oven ready' graduates;

businesses can help more with placements, quality work experience, joint development and delivery of the curriculum. Equally the wider roles of HE need to be better understood and appreciated across Governments so that HE is not just seen as instrumental to the delivery of economic aims but has deeper and lasting values. The education community must better articulate and defend these values. The financial pressures on teaching in particular will continue to require co-funding by the Government, graduates and organisations that benefit from HE. Investing in higher levels of learning is vital if the UK is to be internationally competitive. Participation levels are too low and more younger and older people need the underpinning qualifications as well as aspiration to support their lifelong learning in an increasingly challenging international economic environment. Many more small businesses (whose managers missed out on the still recent expansion of HE) in particular need to make this investment if they and their businesses are to prosper and even survive. For its part, HE has to adapt to meet the forms of learning that are needed by such businesses and by more part-time learners. This will stretch the existing funding, credit, delivery and curriculum models.

The two college representatives, 24 and 37, had more specific suggestions:

Inflexible funding arrangements for directly funded colleges like ourselves limit opportunities for responsive delivery in relation to work-based learning. Not being allowed to access a range of HEFCE funding streams directly, such as the Strategic Development Fund, seriously limits our ability to respond to the employer engagement agenda. Not getting enough ASNs [Additional Student Numbers] to support our growth in HE numbers limits opportunities for non-traditional learners. A further challenge is to lever financial support from employers with regard to fees and delivery costs. Government should consider legislation to secure an employer levy for education and training to develop their workforce. HEFCE and QAA should review their systems and processes in order to enable the HE sector to respond appropriately to the economy's future needs as outlined by Leitch. Otherwise HE growth will be, to quote, Leitch, 'more of the same'. New developments should be based upon new types of programme offering specific, job-related skills such as foundation degrees. HEIs need to be clear as to their role and purpose in relation to the UK's future prosperity. This will allow institutions to work to their strengths and avoid wasteful duplication of effort.

I think the main issue (which we have been grappling with for years) is employer engagement and the answer to this relies on some meeting of HE and employers – a willingness to shift from institutional inertia (on the part of HE) and from a lack of commitment to skills development (from employers). However, the main thing to encourage action is the funding formula which does not either reward innovation or current good practice fairly. The funding system is heavily weighted to traditional institutions and this needs to shift fast to allow the UK to develop truly lifelong learning opportunities for all.

The third suggestion is about acting both to preserve and restore collegiality. Respondent 56 (an administrator in a specialist institution) called for 'more collegiality between top management, academic and administrative staff in order to take missions forward'. Others commented:

My starting point would be to reduce competition and increase cooperation and community locally, regionally, nationally and globally. This would lead to a better quality of life and greater social and cultural equity and positive views of social diversity.
(28 – professor in a specialist institution)

The challenge is to create the kind of spaces in which intellectual engagement is possible. The challenge is to resist narrow forms of managerialism that impede academic enquiry. Directors of HEIs (vice-chancellors, etc.) need to stand up for intellectual values, and show how important these are to society at large, in the face of anti-intellectual ethos of government. They should resist the urge to compete with one another, and manage in ways which are more closely aligned to their academic principles. Government should be much more hands-off and academic staff in general more prepared to resist intimidation.
(45 – professor, Russell Group)

A small minority (note the responses to the questionnaire above) had a silver bullet – scrap fees:

Scrap fees to restore free higher education. (This would mean also restoring progressive taxation to undermine arguments for 'graduate taxes' and fees related to anticipated incomes.)

Transform Oxford and Cambridge into adult residential colleges to make up for all the 30+ year-old students who have been squeezed out of HE by the 18–30 target. Allow entry as of right to local HEIs for all school students graduating at 18 (Oxford Brookes and Anglia Ruskin Unis become the local HEIs for those towns – re previous sentence). Implement the Tomlinson Report's recommendations to replace A-levels with a Scottish higher type qualification combining science, arts and vocational activities. (Re)introduce polytechnic-type curriculum integrated with FE (what Ruth Silver calls 'thick HE'). Research and scholarship/creation as an integral part of all students' Independent Study while allowing publicly funded research institutes, especially for 'big science'.

(30 – 'new' university professor)

A fifth suggestion was a break from quality assurance, QAA and the RAE:

Suspend formal evaluation of teaching and research for two years, so that the first two years after 2008 do not count against any future T or R exercise. Evaluate the results, and reintroduce equivalent systems only if things have got worse.

(39 – 'new' university DVC)

This links with scepticism about the effectiveness of earmarked funding. Here is another 'new' university PVC, correspondent 41:

Accountability to HEFCE and related quangos, and with it connected bureaucracy, is stifling innovation and does not leave enough headroom for creativity. Less purpose specific competitive funding and resulting more mainstream funding, coupled with greater autonomy would benefit the HE sector.

The penultimate 'bullet' is (perhaps predictably) technological: 'Information technology could improve the staff and student experience, and institutions' investment in it needs to be enabled and incentivised, probably by HEFCE' (51).

Finally, several voices got behind the Bologna declarations and their wider ramifications for coordination and exchange across the European Union (EU):

The government also needs to make a substantial commitment to the Bologna process and look seriously at its implications rather than presiding over the half-hearted muddle that we currently have.

(31 – 'new' university dean)

The greatest upcoming challenges arise from curriculum and assessment redesign in the light of Bologna, and how the new fees regime will affect applications for postgraduate study. Emerging markets such as India and China, as well as EU enlargement will present the greatest challenge to successful recruitment of international students in the next decade.

(64 – deputy registrar, specialist institution)

The future of postgraduate education is changing through external demands such as international students and Bologna but also through internal issues such as fees and changing expectations and needs. My role faces the difficulties of meeting these challenges and being able to follow developments and seek to change the agenda constructively or to work with partners to highlight issues.

(70 – sector-wide research leader)

This general optimism is not a popular perception (in both senses of the word). To return to the paradox with which I began this book: perhaps it is a matter of asking the right questions. In this case (and to pervert an important typology) the vast majority of answers are in a kind of 'mode 2' world, recognizing balance, nuance, negotiation and collective commitment at all levels of the organization (Gibbons *et al.* 1994). For how to spring a 'mode 1' (hierarchical and defensive) alternative, Table 4.2 summarizes another point of view. This was generated from an open-ended survey conducted at about the same time for a consultation in memory of the influential and much respected Professor Roy Niblett. Niblett's cue for the exercise was a brief evocation of a university as 'a place at which not only facts and skills are learned but also ranges of thought and feeling, ability to think and feel more deeply but also more controlled than we did before' (Bone and McNay 2006: 3).

What emerged was an example of what I shall call below 'academic populism'. The self-selected group of mostly older academics who responded are the natural constituency of the current international wave of professional dystopians of contemporary HE. If Niblett's vision was under threat, it was others who are responsible.

If you are trying to adjudicate between the two approaches I would say that the 100 voices exercise is methodologically more sophisticated (and more responsible). McNay has a different view (see McNay

Table 4.2   Higher Education and Human Good responses

300+ responses – open invitation
(% agreeing to the propositions below)

- 'Emphasis in universities more on systems than people' – 85
- 'Fear of sanctions against those who speak truth to power' – 79
- 'Pressure from PIs and formula funding has led to leniency' – 75
- 'Research integrity has been compromised' – 70
- HE has 'lost its role as conscience and critic of society' – 72

Source: Bone and McNay (2006)

2007). The age profile of McNay and Bone's sample is relevant: the vast majority are towards the end of their careers. The average age of UK academic staff is now 42.7 (HESA Staff Record 2004–5: Table 23a, see www.hesa.ac.uk). Our modal academic (not Colin and Cheryl, but perhaps Tony or Katherine) was thus born in 1963, entered university in 1983, and possibly got his or her first lecturing job in the early 1990s. By my calculations, something between 132 and 208 of the 274 responses initially analysed by McNay and Bone are older than this (Bone and McNay 2006: 54). To return to the generational discussion in the last chapter, they made their first mobile phone calls in their early thirties and were given a desktop computer in their late thirties or early forties. Then there is the style of questioning. Look at how the statements lead the witness. Note how this is a classic self-selection or 'opt-in' survey: the invitation is now to 'join the petition': no dissent is anticipated, and would clearly not be welcomed (see http://olc.gre.ac.uk/ET/VPPISurvey.nsf).

Another issue that causes as much heat as light is that of 'work–life' balance. Furnham (2004: 159–60) once more reacts with scepticism:

Happiness is a stable trait … What this usually means is those who are unhappy about their work-life balance are likely to remain unhappy irrespective of how the balance is adjusted. People who are unhappy and stressed outside work are likely to remain so however much work hours, responsibility and objectives are altered … The work-life lobby all concentrate on negative spillover. They stress how work makes family life difficult, problematic and unsatisfactory. But it can also do the opposite. It can support, enhance and facilitate life outside the workplace, as the redundant and unemployed soon discover.

This is an extreme, some would say a harsh or complacent, view. But the notion of 'correcting' simple entitlement views of the work–

life equation is increasingly supported by the research literature. In an excellent theoretical review, backed up by two surveys (of working professionals and business school students), Mickel *et al.* establish the extent to which the pursuit of a high quality of life is a dynamic process. Inductively they construct three dimensions of the process: 'having' (e.g. resources of time and money, freedom or flexibility, and health); 'doing' (e.g. the mix of work- and non-work-related activities, the latter including leisure and social responsibilities); and 'being' (e.g. 'connected', 'balanced', 'secure' etc.). The relationships between these zones are bi-directional, can exemplify both positive and negative spillover, and will often be in tension, not least in response to life-changing events. The implications for practice are substantial. Organisations should 'help employees learn to successfully manage their expectations and to negotiate various quality of life tensions'. Employers 'should also have realistic expectations of their employees and clarify them' (Mickel *et al.* 2008).

In the USA, a serious attempt at benchmarking universities' organizational cultures is made by the *Chronicle of Higher Education*'s annual search for 'Great Colleges to Work For', based on a survey instrument devised with the human resources (HR) firm Modern Think. In the first such survey 15,000 respondents from 89 colleges participated. The main conclusion was that 'academics are most upbeat at the beginning and the end of their careers' (Selingo 2008). In the consultants' pitch (see www.modernthink.com):

> In a great workplace, the way people are treated adds significantly to the competitive advantages available to the organization. ModernThink's research covering the nation's best employers for over twenty state recognition programs confirms that these great workplaces benefit from the following:
>
> - Receive more qualified job applications for open positions.
> - Experience a lower rate of turnover.
> - Experience reductions in health care costs.
> - Enjoy higher levels of student satisfaction and loyalty.
> - Foster greater innovation, creativity and risk taking.

How realistic is this nirvana? I return to the question of a 'grown-up' organizational culture in Chapter 6.

The legislative framework ▪

Crudely, the purpose of legislation is to make things better. This can relate to staff morale in a variety of ways. It can offer protection to the vulnerable or it can seek to enhance opportunity. It can secure entitlements, or it can mandate redress. It can be highly specific or general in approach.

A series of statutes, notably the Human Rights Act of 1998, and culminating in the Employment Act of 2002, has progressively incorporated into UK law the provisions of the European Convention on Human Rights (ECHR). Discrimination is now unlawful on the grounds of gender, race, sexual orientation, religious affiliation and age, while in the case of 'public bodies' (including universities) both general and specific 'duties' are identified in respect of race, disability and gender equality. Employment tribunals are currently testing the outer limits of these commitments on the parts of both employers and employees. In terms of the specific role of universities the ECHR – as domesticated in the Human Rights Act of 1998 – has special resonance in its defence of 'freedom of thought' (Article 9) and 'freedom of expression' (Article 10). As Alison Hall points out, in a useful survey aimed at UK university governors, these extend the protections afforded to academics in such statutes as the Education Reform Act of 1988 to 'everyone, including students' (Hall 2009: 5.12). She sets the full context in a useful way:

> There is a very substantial body of primary and secondary legislation applicable to almost all aspects of employment. There is also a significant body of law covering collective consultation with the workforce, and the conduct of industrial relations in unionized workplaces (not to mention the substantial legislative framework around health and safety at work). And that's not all – there are the implications of European legislation too. Private sector organizations must comply with the UK legislation that gives effect to European directives but publicly funded bodies which are regarded as 'emanations of the state' (including HEIs, as a result of both the 'scale of public funding' and the 'impact of government policy on them') must comply with the directives themselves.
>
> (Hall 2009: 1.8, 1.9)

Above all, the legislative framework requires constant attention and vigilance on the part of institutions; and that in turn necessitates professional services. HR departments have become the most solid candidates for that special role as the 'VC's best friend'. They attempted in England to cement this role by positioning themselves centrally in the mandatory 'HR strategies' that HEFCE required in order to secure earmarked funding for 'rewarding and developing staff' (Hall 2009: 1.13).

More informally, HR departments achieve this by persuading the VC that the most important priority for the institution is not to be sued. From the perspective of devolved budget-holders across the university this gives the impression that they are paralysed by fear. Here the stakes are high (employment tribunal damages in cases of 'unlawful discrimination' are now without limits). Locally the impression received is of a 'do nothing outside the guidelines' or 'admit nothing' culture: professionalism as stasis rather than professionalism as facilitation, liberation or support. The 'guidelines' referred to are in the spirit of failsafe engineering, and can lose friends, for example, among recruitment candidates as well as recruiters (the former now receive deliberately bland feedback on failed applications; the latter feel straitjacketed into formulaic procedures). The 'admit nothing' culture means that levels of management back each other's interpretation of what has happened on procedural rather than substantive grounds, resulting sometimes in an escalating defence of the indefensible (and occasionally substantial legal costs).

Meanwhile, independent research has cast significant doubt on HR departments' real contribution to institutions' overall performance, and even suggested that they have contributed to disempowering general and middle managers (Guest and Clinton 2007).

On the positive side, the increasing salience of HR (no longer 'personnel') departments in institutions has led the processes of establishing codified procedures for dealing with issues of, for example, bullying, harassment and grievances, often under the blanket of 'dignity at work'. At the same time HR staff have developed a strong sideline in courses that used to be called 'dealing with difficult people', but have been progressively softened towards 'dealing with difficult situations'. Here is a sample of the objectives of such a course, delivered in my own institution (the IoE), but outsourced to a consultant:

By the end of the workshop participants will have:

- explored the causes and impact of unacceptable behaviours in the workplace;
- raised awareness of personal assumptions and perceptions about individuals;
- developed strategies for dealing with such situations;
- practised strategies with business actors;
- explored the characteristics of effective teams;

- understood the process of team development;
- analysed their strengths and areas for development as team leaders/managers.

Another such course promises 'a practical session for all members of staff, where you will identify and work on assertive behaviours and become more adept at recognising and dealing with behaviours that are less helpful in the workplace'. The 'learning outcomes' anticipated here are as follows:

- To recognise and practicing [*sic*] assertive behaviour at work
- To understand the goals of assertive behaviour
- To clarify the difference between assertive behaviour and other less useful behaviours for getting what we want.

There's no hint of risk or danger in adopting assertiveness as an approach, and such courses have now attracted the interests of satirists more widely. The biggest laugh achieved by the cast of Richard Bean's controversial play on waves of immigration into the Spitalfields area of London (*England People Very Nice* – premiered at the National Theatre in spring 2009) is when the police constable in the Blitz concludes a cadenza of liberal sentiments about the Indian ship-jumping refugee found exhausted in the street by declaring (anachronistically), 'I've been on a course.'

Of wider scope are interests of transparency, of exposure of sleaze, corruption and wrongdoing of any kind. Colloquially these are referred to as 'whistle-blowing', more pompously, 'matters of concern'. Each of these areas will have its associated 'codes' and procedures, and very little incentive once either side has decided to initiate proceedings to call a halt. As with student proceedings there is no provision, generally, for 'a leave to appeal'.

It is often observed that while students have 'complaints', staff members have grievances. This is not the only asymmetry. Staff have no recourse to the Office of the Independent Arbitrator, and since the steady erosion of the powers of the 'visitor' as well as of a 'model statute' (designed exclusively to protect academic staff in chartered universities after the 1988 Education Reform Act from arbitrary dismissal or redundancy) can feel closer to the siren call of legal recourse, earlier than students.

As set out in the 'interim report' of an HEFCE (2008) project on *Improving Dispute Resolution*, English HEIs are subject to at least five levels of injunction and compliance when dealing with actual and potential disputes:

- First there is the law of the land (e.g. the 1998 Public Interest Disclosure Act; it is also important to recognize that HEIs are 'public bodies' for the purposes of freedom of information legislation).
- They are also now 'registered' rather than 'exempt' charities, and have to pay particular attention (under the regulation of the Charity Commission, exercised through the funding councils) to 'charity trusteeship'.
- Then there are the various codes and exhortations covering corporate life in general and the public sector in general (most important here are probably the 'principles' of public service established by the Nolan Committee).
- Then there are the 'entry-ticket' items. For example, signing the Financial Memorandum with the funding council brings along with it the HEFCE's 'public interest disclosure procedure', while the mandatory subscription to the QAA opens up the 'precepts' set out in the 'Cause for Concern Guidance' – for which the current secretary of state wishes to see a 'lower threshold' before the QAA will investigate (Garner 2008). The Research Councils UK (RCUK) not only offer guidance on how to deal with research misconduct but have also established a UK Research Integrity Office (UKRIO).
- Finally, of course there are the things that institutions (necessarily) do to themselves (through procedural and other collective agreements).

Beyond this clearing of this ground, the authors of the report are less helpful. Their goal of establishing a 'whole-institution' approach to dispute resolution is admirable, but their fundamental approach is a populist one. The presumption is that unless trained (in their fashion), 'management' (especially senior managers) will act in an arbitrary fashion, keep governors in the dark, expose the institution to uncapped legal fees, preside over a chaotic administration of unaligned responsibilities (left and right hands) and permanently fire-fight rather than understand what is really at stake.

Of course, any of these pathologies is possible, but so too are the incidences of upwards and sideways bullying, of 'proxy battles' (where what is at issue is quite different from the items on the charge sheet) and of kneejerk counter-suit whenever a charge is mooted or laid.

Digression 3: when grievance becomes obsession

Every institution has at least one unresolved staff grievance that seems to rumble on forever. Another asymmetry rears its head here: the injured party – especially if he or she has left the institution (voluntarily or compulsorily) – has all the time the week brings to advance his or her case. The manager – however well supported – has to deal with this on the corner of an already very crowded desk. As large, well-resourced corporations with professional human relations functions, HEIs can often appear dismissive, arrogant or simply oppressive in these circumstances (there are such cases reflected throughout this book). However, the David vs. Goliath narrative is not invariably true, and can prove damagingly seductive to interested parties, some of which have their own axes to grind.

My own case (heavily anonymized here) concerned a young and very promising scholar in whom the university had invested significantly. There was, however, a record of tension with immediate professional colleagues, including her head of school. Matters came to a head when she explicitly ignored the head's instruction not to travel abroad on a research trip during the first few days of the academic year, when, in her school in particular, it was 'all hands to the pump' to ensure that a complex registration and induction period for new students was worked through. When she returned she was suspended pending a disciplinary inquiry. Following independent professional advice (from her union) she resigned rather than face an inquiry which might have resulted in dismissal. As part of the agreement surrounding the resignation, the university agreed to respond to future requests for references with a positive account of what she had achieved. One week later she requested to withdraw her resignation. Having obtained legal advice, this request was refused. A month later the union sought (unsuccessfully) to reopen negotiations for improved terms and a reference was issued. The resignation took effect.

Things were then quiet for a year and two months. Since then there has been a series of challenges to the university and its senior officers (including the chair of governors). The most important of these have been legal, and have all been dismissed: to an employment tribunal, an employment appeal Tribunal, and twice for judicial review. The final claim was struck out with costs awarded to the university. A legal trail was also accompanied by a series of direct approaches: by solicitors

> threatening reputational damage; by a sector-wide support group accepting without investigation a number of accusations against members of the university (all of which had been tested in the courts and found to be untrue); and by an MP again too busy to investigate the merits of the case but convinced that the small player must be honourable and truthful and the large player the opposite.
>
> The outcome has been more than an inconvenience for the institution (successive new chairs of governors have had to be brought into the argument), but also personal tragedy. Grievance has become obsession and swallowed a promising career.

Several of the parties who became involved in the case set out above thought that it might be susceptible to mediation. The authors of the HEFCE report are sceptical about mediation (unless they are doing it themselves: see the OxCHEPS website for who is available). In fact, for reasons which are uncertain (arrogance, fear of fees and ignorance are possibilities), mediation represents a road rarely taken.

The main players in the field are:

- the Centre for Effective Dispute Resolution (CEDR);
- the Civil Mediation Council (CMC);
- The OxCHEPS mediation service.

I received the following advice about these processes from an expert (Heather Alan, in an interview on 8 February 2007).

> This is not an amateur, do-gooding, 'Lady Bountiful' business. It is hard-nosed and professional (e.g. mediators are trained, accredited and monitored). Only about 75 per cent pass CEDR recognition. There is a strong code of conduct (e.g. on conflict of interest).
>
> The lawyers are the real gatekeepers, generally responsible for calling it in. One party proposes; the other party accepts; the court can recommend. Both sides have to agree, to engage, and (at least formally) share costs (a university might fund both sides, especially in cases involving students or lower-paid employees). The philosophy is neutrality not advocacy. It is totally different from binding arbitration as both sides have to agree. The mediator literally 'doesn't care about the outcome'. The success rate is 70–80 per cent and 65 per cent of agreements are struck on the day.
>
> The approach is 'what would a settlement look like?' The

method is to 'frame and re-frame'. The process is normally pre-meeting; private meetings with parties; a mediation day. The stages are: preparation; opening; exploration; bargaining/negotiation; conclusion and documentation (the latter usually a statement of intent).

Heather's main message was that earlier mediation would be a good thing. In her view HR departments aren't usually very helpful (they are seen to have lost neutrality). David Palfreyman also suggests that mediators can help the plaintiff to be both clearer and more realistic about what a negotiable remedy might consist of (private communication).

'Academic populism' vs. 'new managerialism'

More broadly, what can ensue is a battle between two caricatures. 'Academic populism' is a potent amalgam of unempirical nostalgia, proxy battles (what Baggini 2008: 59–62 calls 'displacement') and arrogance. 'New managerialism' represents an attempt to describe a particularly potent version of 'new public management' as it affects HE, leading to a systematic undermining of 'collegial' values (Deem 1998; Deem and Brehony 2005). Academics feel pressurized, undervalued, misunderstood and poorly led by a new breed of budget- and accountability-obsessed bureaucrats (who are also overpaid). Meanwhile, the managers rail against the unworldliness, self-absorption and economic recklessness of academic prima donnas, who (most seriously) do not take managing anything seriously. The stereotypes are toxic and unempirical (Watson 2000: 6–8).

Both are in stark contrast to what the surgeon Atul Gawande describes as one of his five 'suggestions for becoming a progressive deviant': 'don't complain' (the other four are 'ask an unscripted question', 'count something', 'write something' and 'change'). What he says about doctors may apply equally to academics:

> Doctors are expected to coach themselves. We have no one but ourselves to lift us through the struggles. But we're not good at it. Wherever doctors gather – in meeting rooms, in conference halls, in hospital cafeterias – the natural pull of conversational gravity is toward the litany of woes all around us.
>
> But resist it. It's boring, it doesn't solve anything, and it will get you down. You don't have to be sunny about everything. Just be prepared with something else to discuss: an idea you read about, an interesting problem you came across – even the

weather if that's all you've got. See if you can keep the conversation going.

(Gawande 2007: 249–57)

What happens to 'collegiality' in these circumstances? In 2007 the
HEFCE apparently caused outrage by a suggestion from its Leadership, Governance and Management Committee that (yet another)
'culture change' was required:

> HEIs' staff will need to be more aware of and aligned to the
> strategic needs of the HEI. Academics' goals are often related to
> their discipline rather than their institution and they will need
> to develop institutional loyalties in addition to discipline
> loyalties. Corporate planning processes will need to be com-
> municated more effectively for those processes to be successful.

In the context of a scholarly revival of Humboldtian ideas about
'freedom and loneliness', as well as an account of the 'complexity' of
the university's proper business, Lewis Elton (2008: 232–3) eloquently led the counter-attack: 'I believe that universities are at a
cross road. Either staff loyalty to their institutions will derive from
top down management practice, with a vice-chancellor as a university's chief executive, or institutional management reverts to its
collegial forms, with the vice-chancellor as a university's first
servant'.

If the opposing views are as starkly expressed as this (by both
HEFCE and Elton), the game is probably lost. University leaders have
their own set of paradoxes, about leading both constructive collegiality and corporate purpose. But here is a digression on how we
(currently) find those leaders.

Digression 4: hunting the headhunters

Over the past quarter of a century probably one of the stronger
influences on changing the culture of HEIs in the UK has been
the use of executive search agencies (ESAs), or 'headhunters.'
These are now almost invariably involved in the recruitment
and selection processes for chief executives, and several institutions make a practice of using them for posts well down
the academic and administrative pyramids of management.
Their use can stand as a salutary lesson of what can happen
when the traditional culture of HE meets the potentially brittle
and nervous culture of lay governors.

During the academic year 2006–7 the 152 posts involving ESAs advertised in the *THES* included not only principals and VCs, but other members of the senior management team (deputy and PVCs, registrars and directors of finance), heads of functional areas (estates, HR, library and information services, commercial services, international offices, etc.), deans and professors, but also their deputies and other roles (like 'head of research accounting'). The comments here are mainly about the former (VCs, principals etc.). Table 4.3 shows how ESAs have come to dominate recruitment at this level.

Table 4.3   THES advertisements for institutional heads (1986–2007)

	No. of posts	Posts involving ESAs (%)
1986–7	15	0 (0)
1996–7	16	9 (56)
2006–7	21	20 (95)

Over this period the 'life-cycle' effect has been like that of a sophisticated drug. Initially headhunters had an enlivening and beneficial effect; subsequently the positive effects have worn off and damaging side-effects have emerged. Initially they were expensive and exotic; now they are expensive and routine.

Initially they probably helped in widening the pool of credible applicants, not least by identifying talent from other sectors (including the private sector) and from overseas. They also seriously 'professionalized' the process, for example through applying consistent standards to processes and documentation.

However, to begin with the most serious of the side-effects, fundamentally their use represents a significant outsourcing of essential university responsibilities. There are implications for institutions not doing certain things for themselves. At its worst this can lead to a kind of corporate de-skilling. Interestingly, the UK may not be alone in this concern. In an article in the *Chronicle of Higher Education*, William Bowen, the former president of Princeton, writes about the tendency 'to delegate too much authority to the firm chosen to assist with the search' (Bowen 2008).

This can be especially true (in respect of appointment to chief executive positions) on the part of chairs of governors and other lay members. Chairs, in particular, are under considerable pressure to get it right (and, barring disaster, most only have one shot while in office at doing so). In these circumstances they anticipate receiving a high quality, comprehensive service from the ESA; not least because of the amount of money spent on it. This can lead to intellectual and even moral laziness (the latter, for example, in handing over responsibility for feedback to failed candidates). There is also the 'lay' temptation to privilege messages about the process that come from paid advisers independent of the institution over the potential cacophony of opinion within its walls. This is especially true if lay governors have a perception that problems exist which need to be fixed by new leadership.

At the same time, the headhunters may have had an influence on what are regarded as the essential or desirable characteristics of candidates. For example, there is today a significant emphasis on having been a chief executive before; against which it is at least a testable hypothesis that 'one post' VCs have a better record than *galacticos*.

In practice, collectively the ESAs have created for the sector a kind of competitive waiting room. They earn their money by putting up plausible shortlists. This leads to a tribe of individuals either permanently sitting in the waiting room or constantly being begged and/or seduced to be there. This can be destabilizing for individuals and for institutions. It also leads to the phenomenon (reinforced by the 'feedback' point above) that everyone (except the appointee) 'comes second' – and will therefore be more likely to run again.

One result is that the population of the waiting room is becoming less, not more, diverse. The modal occupant of the waiting room – if not necessarily eventually of the throne – has for some time been a 55-year-old PVC scientist from an old university (David Allen, registrar of the University of Exeter, has recently estimated that there exists a 'hopper' of current and former DVCs/PVCs of between 150 and 200 people, who must spend a significant amount of their time on the phone to headhunters) (Allen 2008). Some of the more interesting potential candidates (younger, female, connected with 'newer' academic and professional fields etc.) are no longer prepared to play again and again, especially if they feel that they have been misled about their 'real' chances in making failed applications. (Hard data on 'long-' and 'short-' lists is, of course, confidential;

but I base these observations on personal participation in the recent selection of eight heads of institutions.)

The headhunter's most compelling unique selling point (USP) is confidentiality. This has one important positive effect: it may get some individuals on the list who would otherwise be reluctant. There are, however, downsides – most seriously the insulation of candidates from any real assessment of the nature and condition of the institution they could be expected to run (elaborate ruses are constructed to keep the candidates apart from each other – and often away from those they will be suddenly asked to lead). This may not help the institution as a whole to choose the best potential leader; it certainly doesn't help the candidate to choose the institution (a reciprocal exercise the importance of which is only too rarely acknowledged). Glynis Breakwell's research for the LFHE on *The Characteristics, Roles and Selection of Vice-Chancellors*, reports that the 13 incumbents she interviewed all expressed deep unhappiness with the process. However, they all claimed to have been invited to put themselves forward: 'people no longer expect to apply for a VC's post' (Breakwell and Tytherleigh 2008).

As for the capacity of the ESAs, how much do they really know about the sector and how it works? Or, for that matter, how well do they understand what exactly it is that its successful leaders do? They seem often bamboozled by reputational hype and by size (e.g. of budgetary responsibilities of candidates in their former roles – as, for example, of deans or senior civil servants, as if these were analogous to whole institutional responsibilities). Some ESAs work only in HE; some predominantly in the 'public service'; some more widely (where they have a touching faith in transferable skills).

Investigating the market among agencies reveals a relatively small, rotating field, which is highly competitive (big players have declined as well as risen, and there is a battle for new entry). In 2006–7, 30 separate agencies advertised a total of 152 posts (at all levels). The clear winners were the Perrett Laver Partnership with 34 (22 per cent).

Although they will protest that this is not the case, individual ESAs must be influenced by the pull of concurrent or prospective assignments ('I'll save this candidate for that job'). They also, of course, have an interest (like footballers' agents) in moving players along.

Of course, most of these negative developments are not the

agencies' fault. A drug trade needs users as well as pushers. The best of the ESAs certainly have a sense of self-awareness about how they can potentially distort the system. They are also responding to a context in which public discourse (and many of the voices to which lay governors will listen) makes a fundamental presumption that there is a leadership deficit in UK HE (this partly explains the desire to look overseas for salvation). Meanwhile they often have to adjudicate some of the contradictions within the institutions: for example, between advocates of hard-nosed managerialism and of academic nostalgia.

How can the sector sensibly disengage or re-group?

One solution is to just say no. A small number of institutions has done just this. *THE* advertised the following posts on 24 January 2008 without reference to ESAs: three PVCs; five deans; deputy and assistant deans; a director of student services; an assistant registrar, and a number of professorial chairs (including one at an ancient university).

Another is to use the firms for what they are good at: research and facilitation. This will involve institutions reasserting their corporate ownership of the process.

Probably most critical is the need to re-create a sense of shared responsibility across the institution, so that, for example, the kind of naïve academic populism about leadership and management that has caused lay chairs and members to retreat into their bunkers and seek enlightenment elsewhere is no longer so influential. For what they are worth, here are my 10 lessons from experience for governors' appointing a VC:

Before the event:

1   Really understand your institutional situation.
2   Define the job.
3   Be open-minded about who could do it.

During the event:

4   Use headhunters strategically.
5   Don't freeze out the community.
6   Remember you are selling as well as buying.
7   Remember why you wanted to be a governor.

After the event:

8   Acknowledge your skeletons.
9   Leave some space for future reward.
10 Insist on a planned transition.

Staff members have a persuasive case for being the ongoing conscience of the university. They remain after students graduate, while governments change, and sometimes after (as Don Aitken, who opened this chapter, pointed out) leaders who have expected (or even demanded?) their loyalty have moved on to pilot larger boats. But this responsibility implies an even larger one: to recognize that for the enterprise to retain and enhance its value, it will need to be more than the sum of their individual (or even in some cases their group) interests. The next chapter explores this concept of a 'stake' more fully.

5

UNHAPPY STAKEHOLDERS

Universities at the beginning of the twenty-first century are perhaps more in the public eye than at any previous time in their history. This leads a variety of interest groups to believe that they have something invested in, and hence some control over, the academy. Well-managed, these 'stakeholder' relationships can be positive and productive. Poorly-managed – on either or both sides – they can result in misunderstanding, the frustration—aggression syndrome, and tears.

Stakeholders: who owns the university?

All around the world today there is a revival of the age-old question (going back famously to Cardinal John Henry Newman) of 'what is the university for?' That is not my question in this book (except indirectly), or in this chapter, for it begs another question, which goes to the heart of governance, leadership and management (as discussed in more detail in the next chapter): 'who decides what the university is for, and how?' There may be several corollaries to this question, including 'why are the wrong people deciding what the university is for?' I want to reduce it to an even more fundamental level. I want to tackle the question of 'who owns the university?'

According to the conventions of corporate governance, organizations are governed in the interests of either shareholders (the institutions, groups or individuals who own the shares – and expect dividends) or stakeholders (the individuals and groups, including the employees, whose interests might be affected by aspects of the organization's performance). To the frustration of several commentators, most universities are neither shareholder nor stakeholder institutions. On one end of a spectrum, institutions with the university title may be wholly for-profit, especially in jurisdictions where the title is relatively unprotected in law. At the other end they may be unmediated emanations of the apparatus of the state. However, in the vast centre-ground they are unashamedly *sui generis*, with, as many commentators have argued, institutional autonomy lying at the heart of the conception of the modern university.

They are also symptomatic of what I think is a breakdown of old-fashioned distinctions between public and private. When VCs are asked whether their institutions are in the public or the private sector, the correct answer is 'yes'. In the early twenty-first century, are there any large, complex businesses which are purely public or purely private?

Here is an exercise I do with students on the MBA in higher education management at the IoE. Where on this spectrum of 'hybrids' does the university sit? Are we most like:

- the Armed Forces (a command structure but very dependent upon outsourcing);
- the Church of England (a consensual community, but one that is legally 'established');
- the National Trust (a private charitable society, but one which guards much of the nation's 'heritage' and acts as a tax-management device);
- the Post Office (a 'privatized' service, with a public 'golden share');
- Banks (private corporations, some now in public ownership because apparently the public cannot allow them to fail);
- the NHS (a constantly restructured devolved service, where individual trusts, although nominally independently governed – especially 'foundation' trusts – can be apparently overruled or reorganized by political *fiat*);
- Schools (a local authority service, but nationally regulated – including through the National Curriculum – but 'governed' on an individual institutional basis); or
- BAE Systems (a private company with a majority of public contracts).

Having run this exercise several times, the results are fascinating. Each alternative has garnered at least some support, including the Armed Forces (because of their need mutually to cooperate) and the banks (where there is a resonance about officially-sponsored mergers). The NHS is the numerical winner overall, boosted by recent discussions in Scotland, where institutions feel that they are under unprecedented political control. Strong minority cases have been made for both the National Trust ('voluntarism' is influential here) and the Post Office (especially because of the drive to keep unions onside). Personally, the correct answer is, I think, closest to the final case (uncomfortable though it might seem at present). We are private corporations, with a lot of important public contracts.

In these circumstances, who owns the university (or pieces of it) or thinks that they do? There are several potential candidates.

The state, directly and indirectly, is invariably a major funder. It will also claim to represent the people's share by investing the proceeds of taxation. However, attempts to co-opt universities into politically-influenced national priorities are dangerous. Nor is it likely to work. Just look at the current agonies of adjustment going on in some of the former eastern bloc states.

Other big investors may be other public services, the professions, business and employers, including through sponsorship and purchase of student places. The 'professions' are a particularly interesting case. They were in at the beginning of the modern European university (law at Bologna; theology at Paris), and they played their part in the nineteenth- and twentieth-century expansion of the system (science and technology in the civics – especially engineering throughout the Commonwealth, and beyond – and more recently the addition of other health professions to the traditional formation of doctors of medicine).

Meanwhile, neighbours also have a point of view. Location is critical. Universities occupy a physical space (including the headquarters and administrators of distance learning outfits). Controversies can include the impact of student and staff presence, but also, from time to time, major strategic decisions.

Digression 5: football and a divided community

Issues that divide the host community may also divide the university community, especially as the latter leave work and go home to join their families and neighbours. Planning disputes show this up in high relief. Planning disputes involving professional football can take it to the edge. Here is one such story.

In April 1997 Brighton & Hove Albion (the Seagulls) played their final league fixture at the Goldstone Ground in Hove. The board of the company had 'realized its asset', which is now a retail park. The club went into exile, initially sharing a ground with Gillingham, and then returning (in July 1999) to take 'temporary' residence in an athletics track (Withdean Stadium) on the edge of Brighton, where they still are.

A campaign began, with strong local authority support, to establish a 'community stadium'. A 'sequential analysis' of potential sites alighted controversially on a site in Falmer, on land partly owned by the University of Brighton and partly by Brighton and Hove Council. Other issues came to intrude, such as the boundaries of the National Park (which could be extended to include the site), a very strong campaign by the local village (Falmer – which has never recovered from being split in two by the adjacent A27), supported by the neighbouring planning authority (Lewes District – whose 'corner' of the site is carefully excluded by the plans), and a referendum on the decision (conducted across the whole of Brighton and Hove – but not Falmer – resulting in a landslide endorsement). A started, stalled and re-started inquiry was eventually 'called-in', caught between the gaps of Whitehall reorganization of departments, and formally challenged by Lewes District Council. It was eventually 'approved' (by the third secretary of state involved) in July 2007. Against this background, a long and difficult set of negotiations took place between the University of Brighton, its neighbour (on the other side of the A27) the University of Sussex, the football club and the council, about planning permissions and agreements and compensation.

The pattern of issues for the University of Brighton included the following:

- a divided community (as suggested above, both inside and outside the university, but also tempered by the need to respect an authentic 'political preference' for the chosen site);
- reassuring the neighbours (especially Falmer village, with which there has been a long history of controversy principally over parking by students and staff);
- university business continuity (e.g. access to a campus which has to operate effectively on evenings and weekends, at the same time as matches could take place);
- organizing the parties to the contract (the university's risks being seen as best mitigated by leasing to the council, which could then sub-contract to the club – and be held responsible for both assurance of the viability of the business plan and its delivery);
- project completion (and sequence – e.g. completing traffic improvements first – the South-East England Regional Development Agency also gets involved here);

- costs (for the alienation of the land, for replacement of the buildings on it etc.);
- ancillary development (appropriate control of the elements the club has to include to make its own business plan work – from both the public and private sectors); and more positively;
- opportunities (including for academic work, such as sports medicine, and the university's own sports programme).

Throughout these negotiations, and in terms of sticking to agreements which undoubtedly bear costs for the developers, the university is under constant pressure: from the club; from the local authority (now with no overall majority, but with all of the committee chairs held by the party in opposition when the game began, and who now wish to convert the adjacent secondary school into an 'academy'); from other parties (including the local FE college, the board of which was chaired by the chief executive of the Club, and which is advised by a former director of finance of the university, and whose expansion plans onto the stadium site form an essential part of the club's business plan); from the media (to which it can constantly be negatively briefed about); from the public (for and against); and from the university community itself (also for and against).

At the time of writing (early 2009) an archaeological consultancy has moved onto the site as a statutory precursor to any development, and enabling work has begun for traffic management improvements (funded separately through the Development Agency). This has been presented to the media as 'beginning work at Seagulls' future football home at Falmer' (it has of course been read as work *on* the Seagulls' future home) (Barrett 2008). Signed agreements exist between the university, the council and the club, about the conditions under which the development can take place, which the university is resolved not to re-open (but which the club will undoubtedly claim must be re-opened to ensure viability).

As a case of managing complex stakeholders; of the stewardship responsibility of governors; of the leadership responsibilities of a senior management team; and of the technical and other demands on university officers (in estates, public relations and sport and recreation, as well as related academic schools), it could hardly be bettered.

Returning to the parade of 'stakeholders', then there is the public more generally, especially as its prejudices are refracted through the media. There are contrasts between the cultural roles of universities and colleges in different national contexts: in the USA they are more loved and respected than may be deserved; in Australia and the UK they stimulate more opprobrium than is objectively fair. This picture may, however, be changing, as US HE is hitting – almost for the first time – a combination of cuts in public subsidy, consumer resentment and consumer debt.

These constitute the various external communities which interact with and within the university.

But probably most important in the historical sense are the internal communities, the members of the university: its staff and students. In his analysis of the downfall of the president of Harvard, Larry Summers, Dean Lewis states that 'in airing their concerns about Summers' leadership, Harvard professors were playing the role of shareholders' (Lewis 2007: 263). I disagree: the appropriate metaphor is surely 'steward'. Simon Caulkin (2009b) points out that in a modern listed company the share register can suffer as much as 90 per cent 'churn' every year.

To describe all of these players as stakeholders is by no means straightforward. Stakeholder is one of those words which has almost exactly the opposite meaning from when it was originally coined (other examples are 'client', 'amateur' and 'maverick'). The stakeholder used to be the person who held the coats – and the prize-money – while the fight was on; the notion was one of scrupulous disinterest. Stakeholders need to understand that if they are to live up to the modern designation (as having invested something themselves), they have to put something at risk. Employers, for example, may reach views collectively (through such bodies as the Confederation of British Industry [CBI] and Institute of Directors [IoD]) that they have few directs means or (in some cases) limited intention of implementing. An example is the aims of the CBI Higher Education Task Force, launched with widespread media coverage in September 2008. In the words of the director-general, Richard Lambert in a press release dated 17 September 2008:

> Clearly, the role of universities is broader than just business, but as a significant funder, user and customer of higher education, it is only right that business sets out what it needs. Our task force will also consider how businesses and universities can work together to ensure that students develop the employability skills business needs, and that more take science, engineering and maths subjects.

It would be interesting to know what levers the director-general thinks he has in this arena: not with the institutions (as there will clearly be a campaign to make the government see that they behave), but with his members (the 'disappointed' businesses).

For a rigorous stakeholder analysis from the perspective of the university throws up some surprising results. It is important to establish first of all whose are the stakes on the table (really) in the sense of sharing risk (individual employers – from the public and private sectors – may well have genuine stakes; the representative bodies will not). Meanwhile, there are arguments about who can most effectively (i.e. legitimately as well as logically) claim to hold the third-party stake (the celebrated 'people's money') on behalf of the community as a whole. The politicians would like to claim it is their prerogative – through democratic validation – although they too can fail the stewardship test, not least through self-serving and short-term policy interventions (see Digression 6 below). And looking inside the institution, what about the wider loyalties of staff: to subject and professional communities beyond their employer's boundaries? And how do students – now aggressively enjoined to act as customers – express their interest?

By any objective analysis of sharing risk, our biggest stakeholders have to be our students. They make the very lumpy investment (usually a lifetime's purchase at each level); they have the most bound up in the lifelong meaning of that investment.

Digression 6: Cassandra and the politicians

The issue of political 'stewardship' is often reduced to one of 'evidence' in policy-making. The late Maurice Kogan's hugely important contribution to HE studies was to argue – and to demonstrate – that the field is of value in its own right. It does not exist as a justificatory or critical tool in the box marked 'evidence-based policy'. Still less should it be empanelled by 'single-issue' advocates of what is wrong or right with the academic estate. Instead, the best HE research seeks to understand a rich internal culture, connected in a wide variety of ways to the environment in which it lives and moves. The resulting work is capable of springing intense and valuable conclusions about human behaviour, organizational effectiveness, and the sources and application of knowledge.

For some of us, this is not enough. All around the world the expectations of HE grow and grow, and they can be contradictory. Universities and colleges are expected to serve governments, economies, societies, groups and individuals in a wide variety of ways. However, the engagement between HE researchers, practitioners and policy-makers can often seem like a dialogue of the deaf.

At their best, the researchers can bring a strong historical sensibility, understanding of the wider role of universities and colleges, and novel insights. At their worst they can be defensive, apologetic, self-serving and repetitive.

At their best, the practitioners (teachers, researchers, managers and support staff of all types) will want to create, validate and use evidence about their practice. At their worst, they will want simply to be left alone.

At their best, the politicians will bring a sense of urgency, resources and democratic validation to the HE enterprise. At their worst they too can be self-serving, but also impatient, simplistic and manipulative.

There are several problems here, including: the problem of *sequence* – when policy choices seem to be made in advance of research-led investigation of the field; the problem of premature *closure* – when policy options are apparently chosen without full consideration of the alternatives; the problem of *over-simplification* – when balanced judgements about a policy choice are presented in aggressively certain terms; the problem of *coordination* – when policies pursued by different arms of the relevant government department, and more seriously in relation to HE by different departments across the government, can confuse and inhibit each other; the problem of *volatility* – when the agencies responsible for policy delivery cannot have confidence that a path once chosen will be consistently and honestly followed for a reasonable period of time; and the problem of *selective attention*. Perhaps most important is the problem of *corporate memory* – when a policy fails to be assessed against the history of the last time it was tried (Watson and Bowden 2005: 7–9).

For example, foundation degrees should surely have been tested as a policy proposition against not only the development of higher national qualifications, but also the experience of the Diploma of Higher Education (DipHE) introduced following the James Report (on the reorganization of teacher training) in 1972. Study of the latter would have shown how a new qualification, designed to engage private sector employers, rapidly transformed itself into a new form of professional accreditation for the public and regulated sectors. In the case of the DipHE the clientele became nurses. For foundation degrees it has been classroom assistants, care assistants, police officers and naval officers. Similarly, many of the rows about the policy of saving money by not funding students taking qualifications equivalent to and lower than those they have already earned (such as the dispute over exemptions, conflict with other goals like prioritizing STEM [science, technology, engineering and mathematics/medicine], and the heavily differential effect on a small number of institutions), could have been anticipated by studying what happened when the policy of 'mainstreaming' adult and continuing education (ACT) was adopted in the early 1990s.

A recent report from the European Science Foundation (ESF) on *Higher Education Looking Forward*, spoke eloquently about its role in 'resolving conflicting social and economic expectations', as well as overcoming 'public myths on the strengths and weaknesses of certain features of higher education'. But it also referred to the 'fatalism' with which research approaches questions like funding and government direction, as something that is consistently being 'done to us' (Brennan *et al.* 2008: 8, 35). HE researchers need to be more than Cassandra; while policy-makers should listen to her more carefully.

Hard questions

If I am right about any of this, then some very big, stakeholder-related questions arise for institutional leadership and management.

The first is about how we use our autonomy.

UK HEIs are – by international comparison – extraordinarily autonomous; and we hold that autonomy at the institutional level. In contrast, autonomy – when it is held, as in some jurisdictions, at the faculty or local level – can restrict institutional freedom of action. However, in the UK we are very ambivalent about autonomy. We pay excessive lip-service to the idea, but we are also hooked on earmarked funding. Lots of university leaders won't do what they know they should unless and until there is a special fund to support it. And they stop as soon as the so-called 'initiative' ends. This can lead to a very curious inversion of institutional priorities. The thing that we assume to be most important becomes not the first but the last call on our institutional resources.

The second is about how we balance our obligations to civil society and the state.

Self-interest can trump stewardship responsibilities and the notion of a wider public interest. At the height of the era of expansion through officially induced competition, our governing boards and councils were basically enjoined to look no further than the bottom line; certainly not to any kind of wider set of interests which might call it into question. And universities can be seduced into an inappropriate relationship with government. University history has some classic cautionary tales here. Perhaps the most dramatic is Heidegger's Rectoral Address to the University of Freiburg in 1933, with its application of Nazi principles to the mission of the university. Richard Wolin shows in detail how, by the time of his resignation in May 1934, Heidegger was 'done in not only by philosophical hubris and his lack of prior political experience, but also by a basic incapacity for political judgment' (2001: 173). The reminder is how we live permanently at the top of a slippery slope.

What, for example, are the underlying implications of decisions being made politically about who is 'under-represented' in HE? What happens to the rest? I could cite cases from around the world on this theme: for example, the Chinese minority in Malaysia (significantly kept out of publicly-funded HE by a legal entitlement of the Malayan majority); Arab-Israelis (apparently especially discriminated against by entrance tests); aspirant national communities in East and Central Europe (where universities have in the recent past played a role in supporting ethnic cleansing); or the issue of language in South Africa (where a tense debate is still underway about whether or not Afrikaans as a medium of instruction perpetuates racial discrimination) (see Watson 2005).

Digression 7: what should go into a new VC's welcome pack?

Following the convention of those fancy hotels, what should a VC find in a basket, wrapped in cellophane, in his or her office on day one?

- I have suggested Heidegger (above) as a reminder of how high the stakes could be.
- In the spirit of stewardship there should also be a letter from the VC's predecessor, giving a frank account of what he or she set out to do, and what remains to be done (the 'skeleton file' of intractable unresolved cases ought to have been discussed earlier – see also the coda below).
- A DVD box set of *A Very Peculiar Practice* – the piece of campus drama that has, in my view, got closest to the

realities of life in a modern university (most of the characters were introduced in a short story, 'Thanks Anyway' in 1990 [Davies 1991: 125–46]).
- A subscription to *The New Yorker* – where you are allowed just to look at the cartoons (sooner or later every dilemma you experience will also appear there).
- A mobile phone with a global chip.
- A bottle of aspirin, a can of deodorant and a packet of handwipes.
- Two pictures of Jack Straw (one as president of the NUS; and one as foreign secretary, leader of the House of Commons or secretary of state for justice).

The third hard question is about how institutions treat each other (the other members of the sector).

What lies behind much of the historical success of the UK sector is the concept of a controlled reputational range. It is important that institutions at each end of the reputational pecking order can recognize each other, and have something tied up in each other's success. The self-appointed 'gangs' in the system (the Russell Group, the 94 Group, Million+, the 'Alliance' and Guild HE) don't help much in this respect. For them, 'autonomy' is mostly bound up in getting a third party (the government) to restrict the freedom of manoeuvre of their rivals (a key example is the manoeuvring that takes place after each RAE – for which 2008 is no exception).

The fourth is about how handle the 'Russian Doll' (or 'onion skin') question of service simultaneously to the neighbourhood, the sub-region (which may be a city), the region (officially and unofficially defined), the nation, the international region (like Europe) and the global enterprise of HE. 'Stakeholders' will exist at all of these levels.

Starting with the local, until the advent, in the late twentieth century, of company or for-profit universities, all university institutions grew in some way from the communities that originally sponsored them. These acts of foundation varied according to a range of local circumstances, in time and location. Many such founding commitments have been transformed – positively and perversely – over the ensuing years; it is revealing, for example, to look at the charters of the Victorian and Edwardian 'civics' (where local and regional themes abound). In this context, the familiar image of a university as somewhat separate from its community – as, for example, an ivory tower – is curiously unfaithful to the historical record.

Understanding the 'pattern' of university foundations is essential.

So, too, is the use of founding purposes – however and how far they need to be updated – in testing university strategic choices. Understanding their institution's history is an important part of any university management's drive to contribute to contemporary society, including on a global scale. At Birkbeck College, I am told that the senior staff, when faced with a difficult issue, ask 'what would George [Birkbeck] think?'

Meanwhile, at the more expansive end of the scale, simplistic analyses of whether we are 'winning or losing' in a global marketplace undervalue the historical role of HE internationally, which has been much more profoundly structured around cooperation and mutual support than competition and nationalistic breast-beating. They can also be allied with a naïve, melioristic view of globalization.

From the ethical point of view there are questions about the mutual support between national systems of HE at different stages of development; about the asset-stripping of key personnel; about a potentially pre-emptive 'western' model of intellectual property registration; and about 'dumping' of poor quality e-learning materials. This is not the kind of 'market' that works simply by driving out all of the competition (Watson 2007b: 32–3).

The final question is about how best to preserve the 'ethical idea' of the university.

There is a kind of presumption that, as 'stewards' of responsible knowledge creation, testing and use, universities are expected to behave well. Most of the preconditions for behaving well seem to rely on aspects of 'emotional intelligence' at all levels of the institution, as well as serious corporate self-study. They include establishing and nurturing a grown-up internal culture (as discussed further in Chapter 6), avoiding the naïve extremes of academic populism on the one hand and management triumphalism on the other. This in turn relies on a secure institutional grasp of the corporate strategy (what is called in some charters and governing articles 'character and mission'). Institutional insecurity – notably financial – can quickly fracture common purpose (to put the point crudely: getting the money right is a necessary but not sufficient condition of institutional success). There is also a need for a general sense of responsibility for what is done in the institution's name – from marking to marketing; from ethical research to being a good neighbour.

The terms of exchange are similarly important: mature institutions cultivate a discourse that neither over-claims nor over-blames. They also maintain a culture in which intellectual excitement, joy (and even fun) coexist with a sense of responsibility and even mercy (not all academic exercises – on the part of individuals and groups – should be expected to succeed). In other words, they choose to behave well – towards all of their legitimate stakeholders (Watson 2008).

It is a shared understanding of the quality and standards of our academic processes that places institutional autonomy in context; that reassures the institutions of civil society and the state about our intentions and their outcomes; that threads together the diverse parts of an HE sector; that confirms the currency of our awards at local, national and international levels; and that reminds us what it is – in our core business – to behave *well*.

So what (finally) is the answer to the over-arching question in this chapter: who *does* own the university? One answer is very simple, it is the university itself: the members of the corporation or of the governing council. They have the powers that are traditionally associated with ownership. Another answer is harder and more ambiguous: it stretches away from narrow ownership horizontally (or as the social scientists would say, synchronically) in terms of all of those other parties who share our risks; and vertically (or diachronically) forwards in time – our governors are temporary stewards of an enterprise with goals that will outlive them. And our members' morale will depend significantly on understanding and feeling comfortable with their place in the scheme of things.

As a result, nobody owns the university forever, and everybody can own the university from time to time. Identifying the stakeholders, inside and outside of the organization, is a critical part of any university's programme of self-study and self-knowledge. The next chapter will discuss the implications of this insight for the management of morale.

MANAGING MORALE

'Managing morale', like 'teaching leadership', sounds like an impossible task. In the former case you can't just tell people to feel better; in the latter you can't fundamentally change people's personalities. However, you can create conditions in which performance improves in both respects: in which morale is likely to be more constructive and in which leaders are able and willing to learn. Without being sentimental or naïve about this, I would contend that some HEIs have this quality and others do not; and that you can sense which type you are in after no more than a couple of days of walking around (a recent survey of staff stress found 'wide variation' and 'highly significant differences' between high- and low-scoring universities) (Auty 2008).

As suggested right at the beginning of this book, VCs and other leaders can go looking for happiness or unhappiness within their institutions, and what they find may well depend upon how they go looking for it. Sooner or later, however, a lot of it will come across the leader's desk: in internal mail, in external mail, via the telephone or email. What can we learn from the VC's postbag?

Digression 8: the 'green ink file'

In 1968 I was an undergraduate at Cambridge, reading history, and full of revolutionary zeal after a year of teaching in a secondary school in Julius Nyerere's then admirably idealistic Tanzania. Master of my college and VC of the university was Sir Eric (later Lord) Ashby. Thinking back to that period (1968–71), a lot of the lessons which have subsequently proved most useful to me in leadership roles in HE were learned from Ashby (for a scholarly account of Ashby's immense contribution to the wider HE world see Silver 2003: 151–73, for his still highly relevant analysis of the academic estate see Ashby 1959: *passim*).

One such lesson, which is very hard to emulate, was the power of relentless courtesy. Another (easier emotionally, although more time-consuming) was his approach to his mailbox. He showed me how he went through it all, every day, moved on the business which he could, and ensured that everybody who needed to know understood the position he had reached on the more difficult items. This was an early version of what Robert Reich, Clinton's secretary of labor, describes as the three-tray model: 'in', 'out' and 'too hard'. Ashby's 'holding notes' were masterpieces, and more than a match for the revolutionaries' 'non-negotiable' demands. We were invariably defeated by lunchtime.

As VC, I made a point of always seeing everything that arrived in the University of Brighton addressed to me, however rapidly it was then sent on or filed under the desk. I found this pile of paper to be an indispensable source of information about what was really going on. Meanwhile, although responsibility for the vast bulk of routine responses, and for dealing with the nuances of most of the 'too hard' items, quite properly lay elsewhere, this self-screening worked. It helped to eliminate unwelcome surprises and it gave me a sense of what was being done on my behalf and on behalf of the institution.

There were also some other delights. There is a fascinating range of goods and services that organizations think the university needs. There is the hard sell (my favourite was the periodic pitch about 'the benefits of a private business jet' – which I passed straight on for the chairman's consideration). There are the promotional efforts on behalf of the apparently irresistible employee, the apparently perfect overseas agent, or the advocate of a curriculum approach the adoption of which will ensure world peace in no time at all.

More seriously, there is the human factor. Praise for the university, its staff and students, is always welcome, but it is also important to have a handle on the range and nature of expressed disappointment, anxiety or complaint. In response, the timely apology, an explanation of what can now be done by way of investigation and potential redress – and in some cases a measured but firm refutation – can reduce subsequent confusion and misplaced expectations. The art of the holding reply, or the value of an early and clear statement of a sticking point, are both rapidly learned by experience. So, too, is how to identify the lunatic fringe (we always called this the 'green ink' file).

In terms of light relief, there was also the variety of forms of address. Over 15 years, my name, title, gender, role, qualifications and postal address were all wonderfully garbled, including by organizations who you would think ought to know better. I was identified as the 'financial director', 'the chief officer', 'the one in charge', the 'head teacher', the 'principle' (a *THES* survey once identified our collective noun as 'a lack of principals'), the 'rector magnificus and president'; and more surreally as the 'ice-chancellor', the 'vic-chancellor', plain 'vice', and (my favourites) 'Mr University' (by Vodafone) and 'St David Watson' (by the Royal College of Midwives).

Ashby, of course, did not have email, and thereby hangs another story. As VC, I never had that screened either, and rather enjoyed the idea that anyone in the university could get a message through my desk. But that was before spam really took hold. I'd like to think that I don't need the offers of specialist pharmaceutical aids which now represent 10 per cent of my inbox, and I know that former members of West African governments don't really need my assistance in getting their money out of the country (not too recently a Russian university fell for this one). I'd rather muse about which UK VC will be the first to rent that executive jet.

Story-telling ▐

It is fashionable to refer to the process of institutional self-knowledge as 'story-telling'. Story-telling in complex organizations received a big boost at the turn of the century from Steve Denning's book about the World Bank, *The Springboard: How Story-telling Ignites Action in Knowledge Era Organisations* (further elaborated in Denning 2005). It is, however, quite important not to look at stories in organizations through rose-tinted spectacles. Don't assume that all story-telling in institutions is good (or that the same is true about institutional humour – Rob Cuthbert has written powerfully on this); it can also be corrosive and disruptive. 'The principal is the shepherd of his people; the vice-principal is the crook on his staff' (see Cuthbert 1996: 97). Denning's latest work has an important section on 'taming the grapevine' (Denning 2005: 201–23).

In story-telling, the 'management' trick is probably the maintaining the connection between the big story and all of the little stories that parts of the organization like to tell (about their students, themselves and their achievements). It doesn't mean that the big story and all of the little stories have to be the same. It may even be tolerant of contradictions between the big story and the little stories (i.e. 'tolerance' may be part of the big story itself). From a wider perspective, Gerald Delanty says almost the same thing: 'there is no single legitimating idea of the university, no grand narrative, but a plurality of ideas and a growing diversity of universities and institutions of higher education' (Delanty 2008).

Digression 9: harmony and counterpoint, conducting and captaincy

Musical composers have always known how to tell several stories simultaneously. There are many examples: the *stretto* in a classical fugue; the combination of *leitmotif* that writers of programme music employ (think of Richard Wagner, as most clearly demonstrated in the Overture to *Die Meistersinger*). Then there is Charles Ives' Second Symphony, as described here by Alex Ross (2008: 132):

> Ives opens the old Teutonic form to what the musicologist J. Peter Burkholder calls 'borrowed tunes': American hymns, marches and ditties of the order of 'Massa's in de Cold Ground', 'Pig Town Fling', 'Beulah Land', 'De Camptown Races', 'Turkey in the Straw', 'Columbia, the Gem of the Ocean'. These swirl together with quotations from Brahms, Wagner, Tchaikovsky, and Dvořák himself, provocatively levelling the European-American balance.

The closest late twentieth and early twenty-century inheritor of Ives' mantle is probably John Adams (composer of the suite 'My Father Knew Charles Ives' [he didn't, but he ought to have]). In his autobiography Adams points to a similar creative approach through appropriation and juxtaposition (an approved version of what Jason Frand – quoted in Chapter 2 – would call 'consumer/creator blurring'). In *Harmonielehre* (the work with which he was firmly established, and whose title is also borrowed – from Schoenberg):

The harmonics brush up against many totemic works of the preceding hundred years, from *Parsifal* and *Pelléas and Mélisande* through the Mahler of the Tenth Symphony to Sibelius (particularly his Fourth Symphony) and the luminescent, crespuscular tone-painting of Schoenberg's *Gurrelieder*. There was a playfulness, even an impudence about my ease with appropriation. The music reveled in a kind of enlightened thievery that I would never be able to commit later.

(Adams 2008: 130–1)

Perhaps a popular apogee of sorts is reached when Meredith Wilson, composer and lyricist of *The Music Man*, manages to make the big tunes of both the first and second halves of the show ('Goodnight My Someone' and 'Seventy-Six Trombones') fit together.

The VC's role is often likened to the conducting of an orchestra. Bringing out the contributory themes is a specific example of what this could mean.

Another popular metaphor is the captain of a sporting team, but here too the picture is more subtle than it is usually presented. Ed Smith, the cricketing author of *What Sport Tells Us About Life*, seeks the advice of the film-maker Stephen Frears, who in turn points to the now legendary former England captain, Mike Brearley:

'You are trying to create a kind of benign dictatorship – although I use the term reluctantly,' Frears added. 'You are paid to make decisions, you can't avoid that. It's mostly about bringing the best out of other people. And beneath the surface, of course, you are dealing with the actors' unconscious, alongside your own unconscious – all on a day-to-day level. That's the Mike Brearley position.

Film-making as leadership; captaincy as leadership – the idea obviously intrigues Frears. 'Brearley had the ability to be present and yet somehow absent at the same time … What I admire, and you see it particularly in players who might be past their prime, is the feeling that what they have lost physically they make up for by seeing the whole picture. They grasp the shape of the game, they can somehow stand above it and see it clearly.'

(E. Smith 2008: 164–5)

There are echoes here of F. Scott Fitzgerald's adage in his un-finished Hollywood novel, *The Last Tycoon*, about how few are those who can grasp 'the full equation'. Incidentally, I hasten to say that I offer these metaphors in a spirit of entertainment only (from which they all derive). I am with the fierce *Financial Times* columnist Lucy Kellaway in her condemnation of any 'theory' based on them. The latest candidate for such treatment is apparently boxing (endorsed by the *Harvard Business Review*). As Kellaway (2009) concludes: 'We know what we need to survive in troubled times and it does not take 11 pages of boxing parallels to tell us ... There are two things that we don't need to do: float like a butterfly or sting like a bee'.

Despite this stricture, it is worth thinking about the conditions of a successful big story.

- *Authenticity* is one element. It has to be believable. Of how many claims to be 'world class' is this true? Or how persuasive are the ubiquitous claims in undergraduate prospectuses to lead the sector in this or that.
- Its authors have to be in control. Hence *autonomy* is important. Telling a story you have been given by someone else is likely to lack conviction.
- It may well have to be *adaptable.* The most successful universities and colleges have always been good at re-inventing themselves; or, to put the point more crudely, at keeping their options open (sometimes seen negatively as 'risk aversion'). Put more positively, as Gerald Delanty (2008) affirms, the university is a 'process' (or, as I would prefer to call it, a 'work in progress'), rather than a 'form or a structure'. Ron Barnett, as usual, has a nice conceit for this: 'a mosaic on the move'.
- Above all, it has to be based on an understanding of what is really going on. It has to be *analytical.* Self-study is vital (Watson and Maddison 2003). What is more, the analysis has to be 'inside-out' as well as 'outside-in'. We can spend too much time on what is being done to us, and not enough on what we are doing to ourselves.
- None of this, of course, precludes the story being appropriately *ambitious.* It is just that the ambition has to be grounded.

What can frustrate university leaders is a sense that they are not in control, as they imagine their counterparts in the private corporate world to be. On this score there is some reassurance from the

Stanford Business School. Jeffrey Pfeffer and Robert Sutton include the illusion that great leaders are in control of their companies among their collection of *Hard Facts, Dangerous Half-Truths and Total Nonsense*. In reality, they conclude, 'believing you are in control can wreck your organization'. Instead what good leaders should do is to build systems and teams, 'figure out when and how to get out of the way', project confidence, 'be specific about the few things that matter and keep repeating them', and 'if all else fails, slow the spread of bad practice' (Pfeffer and Sutton 2006: 206–30). The celebrity VC, who attempts to build an organization in his or her image, is empirically (eventually) doomed. Constructively, Pfeffer and Sutton's final injunction is that leaders should promote curiosity: 'Leaders breed such curiosity by having both the humility to be students and the confidence to be teachers (and to know when and how to switch roles) (2006: 234).

To return to stories, the current fashion is for creating HE 'scenarios'. Everyone in the UK is doing it, from our governments through the funding councils to the institutions themselves. The results, in my view, are pretty feeble. There are only really four scenarios:

- The first is IT-driven: *the wireless/wired universe*. Everything and everybody is connected to everything and to everybody else.
- The second is political-science driven: *the new Cold War (with increasing hot spots)*. Islamic faces Christian fundamentalism, leavened by north-south polarization.
- The third is economically driven: *the victory of the Asian tigers*. This is a kind of reverse colonialism. We will end up by feeding their economies.
- The fourth is from environmental science. We have destroyed the balance of the globe through greed and lack of foresight. Global warming means that *we shall either drown or fry*.

Cleethorpes College has to decide by Thursday which of these it will be dealing with in five years time.

This process reminds me of Christopher Booker's famous thesis that there are only really seven stories in the whole of literature:

- overcoming the monster;
- rags to riches;
- the quest;
- voyage and return;
- comedy;
- tragedy;
- rebirth (Booker 2005).

Applying this to the story of your own institution, which one are you?

In October 2008 I asked 40 MBA higher education management students to write the 'story' of their institutions in 50 words or less (a little more than a classic 'elevator pitch', more like the walk from the car park with a distinguished visitor). The results were reassuringly fresh, attractive and free of both jargon and bombast. Here are two very different examples.

X was founded in 2002 as a private-public partnership by the university [of X], banks, law firms and regulatory bodies. Its mission is to provide an education to future leaders in the finance sector as well as serving as a think-tank for financial matters and as a centre for exchange between the legal profession and academia.

Y was formed from four teacher-training colleges, three with religious origins and became a university in its own right very recently. It is located on its own campus on the periphery of a major city, and recruits mainly to social science, liberal arts and education undergraduate programmes.

One very short story was so distinctive in its haiku-like qualities (it is one syllable short) that it defied analysis alongside the rest: 'Married – beheaded – died – married – beheaded – survived'. The author was happy for it to be identified as Thames Valley University.

In terms of the overall approach, the following features stood out:

- 21 of the 40 (53 per cent) spent several of their available words on a fairly detailed history of the institution's foundation and subsequent development;
- 12 (30 per cent) stressed the change of status or purpose of the institution over time;
- 12 (30 per cent) referred to location or place (either generally – a region or the urban environment – or specifically);
- another 12 (30 per cent) described subject mix in some detail;
- 7 (18%) made a virtue out of size (either big or small, with only one declaring itself to be 'medium-sized').

I also checked for frequency of nouns, adjectives and adverbs. In this I disregarded proper names, places and dates as well as the following ubiquitous terms: 'founding/foundation' ,'mission', 'college/ university/polytechnic', 'study' and 'education/educational'. Of what remained, perhaps unsurprisingly, 'research' headed the list,

Table 6.1 'Story-telling' – frequency of terms (% of stories)

- 23 (58%): 'research'
- 13 (33%): 'teaching'
- 11 (28%) 'students'
- 12 (20%) 'business/industry/enterprise'
- 8 (20%) 'cities' or 'regions'
- 8 (20%) 'community/civic/social/neighbours'
- 5 (13%) 'professions'
- 4 (10%) 'employment'
- 4 (10%) 'religion' (in various forms)
- 4 (10%) 'women'

followed by 'teaching', and two sets of terms reflecting 'service'. The leading results are in Table 6.1.

While students scored reasonably highly, with 11 specific references (28 per cent), staff had only three (8 per cent). In terms of current discourse (or political correctness), it was surprising that 'employment' only received four hits (10 per cent); 'quality', 'partnerships', 'status' and 'environment' only three hits each (8 per cent); 'innovation/innovative', 'networks', 'change', 'collaboration', 'creativity', 'diversity', 'Europe', 'excellence', 'management', 're-putation', 'skills' and 'values' only two each (5 per cent); and 'risk', 'accessible', 'choice', 'widening participation', 'league tables', 'inter-cultural', 'knowledge', 'opportunities', 'regeneration', 'satisfaction', 'scholarship', 'stakeholder', 'standards', 'target' and 'trust' only one each (3 per cent). The leading self-evaluation terms were 'interna-tional/world/global' at 15 (38 per cent), 'high' or 'highest' at 12 (30 per cent), and 'focus/focused' at six (15 per cent). Other interesting adjectives were: 'affordable', 'beautiful', 'challenging', 'comfortable', 'flexible' (twice), 'happy', 'incremental', 'independent', 'interesting', 'inward-looking', 'local', 'narrow' (twice), 'national', 'oldest', 'out-spoken', 'perfect', 'personal', 'philanthropic' (twice), 'pioneering', 'planned', 'poor', 'practical', 'respected', 'specialist', 'stimulating', 'top' (three times), 'tremendous', 'unhappy', 'urban' (twice), 'vi-brant', 'well-known' and 'young' (twice).

Digression 10: I do like to be beside the seaside

Here is a contrasting account of a synthetic exercise in story-telling. In 2007, in response to a conference on the fate of seaside communities, I worked with Brian Ramsden, founding chief executive of the Higher Education Statistics Agency

(HESA) and author of the UUK Longer Term Strategy Group's series *Patterns of UK HE Institutions*, to construct another HE 'gang' to sit alongside the existing self-selected groups. These now include:

- the Russell Group (20 members);
- Million+ (formerly the Campaign for Mainstream Universities and before that the Campaign for Modern Universities) (32);
- the 1994 group of 'smaller research-intensive universities' (19);
- Guild HE (formerly the Standing Committee of Principals) (21); and the latest,
- the University Alliance (declaring itself, with no irony at all, to be the successor to the group of 'non-aligned universities') (23).

In constructing the fictional 'Association of Seaside Universities' (ASS), we deliberately avoided those in very large port cities (but we did retain Swansea – being right on the beach); we also cheated in respect of tidal inlets (as in the two Dundee institutions). What we were after was a group for which the 'seaside town' context would have a real affective meaning and could enable contrasts with other similar conurbations without university-type institutions (the archetypical contrast would be between say Brighton and Bournemouth on the one hand and Blackpool and Scarborough on the other). Our sample was as follows:

- University of Aberdeen
- University of Wales, Aberystwyth
- University of Abertay, Dundee
- University of Wales, Bangor
- The Arts Institute at Bournemouth
- Bournemouth University
- The University of Brighton
- The University of Dundee
- University College Falmouth
- The University of Plymouth
- The University of St Andrews
- The University of Sussex
- Swansea Institute of Higher Education
- University of Wales, Swansea

On this basis, the ASS would have 14 substantial university-type institutions and 7.1 per cent of all of the students in UK HE. It is noteworthy that four are in Wales and five in Scotland. Compared to the rest, collectively they have:

- a higher concentration of first degree students (62 vs. 56 per cent);
- a smaller proportion of postgraduate students (20 vs. 22 per cent);
- a lower propensity to study part-time for first degrees (10 vs. 12 per cent);
- a higher proportion of female students (59 vs. 57 per cent);
- about the same proportion of 'other-EU' students (5 per cent); but
- a lower proportion of non-EU international students (8 vs. 12 per cent);
- a slightly higher proportion of female staff (37 vs. 36 per cent);
- a slightly older average age of staff (43.2 vs. 42.7 per cent);
- a stronger tendency towards the arts and humanities (although health and biological sciences are also stronger than the average, as is law); and
- students with a significantly stronger tendency to be occupying their own (owned or rented) accommodation (55 vs. 42 per cent).

Funding council income is 44 per cent of the institutional income compared with 39 per cent nationally. Funding council teaching grant is 7.9 per cent of the total, but fee-income only 6.4 per cent of the total.

Eliminating the big players undoubtedly does have an effect here. The aggregate data does suggest a slightly tired, off-the-pace pattern of provision, contradicted I think by the concentration of art and design and its central role within the creative economy. If you play the 'branding' game, what TV series is your university like? The answer is likely to be the *Golden Girls* and *Dad's Army* meets *Friends* and *The Young Ones*. The most statistically suggestive feature is the final one, which undoubtedly has something to do with the private rental economy in resort towns (including its historically seasonal nature).

I shared this data with the then heads of the institutions (several have subsequently moved on, and some institutions have changed their status and/or title), and asked them for 'any quick reflections … on the importance of the seaside location for the mission and performance of [their] institutions'. Here are some of the responses.

University of Abertay: Professor Bernard King
Dundee does have a seaside bit, but is really (in origin) a fortified port. The only really university seaside places I can think of are Aberystwyth/St Andrews/Bournemouth/Brighton, in the recreational sense.

   Despite all of this, we share most of the attributions of your seaside group, except part-time postgraduate students, female students, and arts and humanities focus, but that is really because we are founded as an 'industrial' university, not a seaside one.

University of Wales, Aberystwyth: Professor Noel Lloyd
The location of Aberystwyth provides a very attractive setting for the university and enhances the overall student experience. It provides a range of outdoor activities which would not otherwise be available.

   In terms of the university's academic provision, it provides valuable facilities for our specialisms in environmental and marine biology.

University of Wales, Bangor: Professor Merfyn Jones
I believe our proximity to the sea is significant to us in two very different ways.

   Firstly, it allows us to engage in teaching and research in marine biology, marine zoology, oceanography and related subjects, largely based at our School of Ocean Sciences (although there is also activity elsewhere). We also have a thriving third mission arm, the Centre for Applied Marine Studies, and through a joint venture, we also have our own £3.5 million ocean-going research ship, *Prince Madog II*. So as you can see, our location on the coast underpins a significant part of our academic activity.

   Second, it is clear that our location on the Menai Straits means that our campus and facilities are located in a rather spectacular environment which is very attractive for students and their parents, and for staff, though I should add that our proximity to the mountains of Snowdonia National Park is equally important.

Having graduated at Sussex and worked at Swansea and Liverpool universities before coming here to Bangor, you can see that 'seaside' universities have played rather a large role in my career!

The Arts Institute at Bournemouth: Professor Stuart Bartholomew
The Arts Institute would match the profile you have drawn with the exception of the proportion of European/international students. For our part this is 15 per cent. With regard to rented and owned there are likely more in the latter category although parents are frequently the title owner.

The concept of seaside is of course spatially accurate but it conveys an image of UK at leisure circa 1935. I prefer 'coast' although my marketing colleague uses 'beach'. Beach has been a significant draw for us here and probably because we have a rather good one. However, beach is not for sitting on, it is the launch pad for surf, sail and let's be frank, sex.

What universities and colleges have contributed to seaside communities is a new local industry which has, in turn, attracted other new industries and cultural activity. They have been regenerative in areas of decline.

Bournemouth University: Professor Paul Curran
Interesting data; some of the differences are very small and are I suspect, primarily the result of there being no big civics at the seaside. I offer three comments that may be helpful.

- We survey our students regularly and the reasons they select Bournemouth University (after 'the right course') are, in order: career prospects, reputation and lifestyle. The main component of 'lifestyle' is the social life but a 'surfing-type lifestyle' is undoubtedly important for some.
- Our seaside location has helped the development of our academic reputation in fields as diverse as tourism and environmental science.
- It is interesting to ask if there are particular characteristics that are unique to seaside universities. If so then I would expect that both (i) our student's second choice university and (ii) the university selected by students who declined our offer, would tend to be located at the seaside. Neither is the case. In both situations the selected university is primarily within the wider region where a minority are seaside universities.

The University of Dundee: Sir Alan Langlands
Not so much the Russell Group, more the Mussel Group?

I'm not sure that the University of Dundee qualifies as a 'seaside university', having a stunning estuarine situation rather than its own beach. However, in the spirit of most applications in the HE sector we're quite prepared to challenge the membership criteria and make a pitch on widening access to tidal estuaries.

Undoubtedly the most important bonus of having a 'seaside aspect' to the university is the stunning views and their promise of a superb quality of life. Many a high-flying appointment has been 'clinched' in the principal's office at the University of Dundee looking out over the sparkling waters of the Tay as the sun plays on the waves and the odd academic billows past in a flurry of surf and sail. Rowing, sailing, kayaking, windsurfing, beachcombing, swimming (for the bold) and simply strolling about on the sand can be as powerful in attracting staff and students as the best research and teaching ratings – to which, of course, Dundee also aspires.

Coastal and estuarine science is an area of special interest here too, where remote sensing, fluid dynamics, geomorphology, environmental management and aspects of aquatic sciences can all be studied in situ. Water law and policy – an issue of crucial global importance – is a major strength at Dundee where, last year, we established the UK's first UNESCO centre and the world's first centre specializing in water law and policy.

The seaside or estuarine effect can be surprising in its ramifications. One of our leading researchers into gut bacteria claims his first inspiration for the importance of microbes in the digestive system lay in gazing at a handful of Tay Estuary mud.

University College Falmouth: Professor Alan Livingstone
Your question is timely as we are currently reviewing our strategic plan with a view to submitting a new version to HEFCE in July this year.

I would start by saying that our immediate environment is a critical element of our USP and one we forefront as part of the student experience at Falmouth. We've highlighted this through our promotional campaigns using 'space' as a trigger – space to think, space to create – emphasizing how our location can stimulate creativity. This is also reflected in our academic provision, for example, marine photography. Our location provides a context and is having a stronger influence on our developments – reference the carbon neutral debate and staff research interests.

There is a strong link between the college and the local community (Falmouth and Cornwall). This symbiotic relationship has developed over the years. One example is student occupation of holiday accommodation out of season. This connection has strengthened more recently as the college and the community has benefited from European funding (reflecting Cornwall's status as the poorest county in England). The college has a genuine and developing sense of responsibility to its community. This social obligation is high on our list of strategic drivers.

University of St Andrews: Dr Brian Lang
We survey our students regularly, to seek their views on their experience in St Andrews and to ensure we are giving them the level and quality of service that they can reasonably expect. We ask them what they appreciate most about St Andrews. The low staff/student ratio? Being taught by five-star researchers? The intellectual challenge? The international staff and student community? Every time, the top rated amenity is 'the beach'.

University of Sussex: Professor Alasdair Smith

1   I'm sure that being in the kind of seaside town that has, or used to have, a tourist trade has a big impact on the range of accommodation available to students, so I am not surprised to see that seaside universities have more of their students in their own accommodation.
2   Location is important to Sussex, but being 50 miles from London is probably more important to us than being 3 miles from the sea. Not a mission issue in the sense of teaching vs. research; but a very important aspect of our location in the undergraduate student market, where state schools in north London are the heart of our market. And a significant issue for staff recruitment, especially in a world of dual-career families.
3   There are many characteristics of Brighton that are very important to Sussex, and the fact that it is a gay-friendly place is (I think – and this is entirely subjective) a very positive factor for us in relation to staff recruitment while only a minor factor in relation to student recruitment.

Whether this has anything to do with it being a seaside town, I leave to those with more knowledge of cultural geography than I have.

University of Wales, Swansea: Professor Richard Davies
We use our location 'in a park by a beach' in much of our promotional material, from prospectuses to further details of academic posts. As a statistician, I set rather high standards for 'convincing evidence' and would have some professional difficulty justifying rigorously the following claim, but I nevertheless believe it wholeheartedly: our location is a significant factor in attracting both students and academic staff to Swansea. We are benefiting from an increasing interest in quality of life and living in a pleasant environment.

In a recent press interview, I stated that 'every day I drive towards the university, looking across at the sun (usually) sparkling across the bay, and then turn into a campus in a park. I must be the luckiest VC alive'.

I hope this is helpful even if data free.

Swansea Institute of Higher Education: Professor David Warner
From our point of view, we have certainly failed to capitalize on our location (both seaside and the first area of outstanding natural beauty to be designated in the UK – The Gower). Similarly, Swansea City & County has also failed to capitalize on this, but has recently established a company to promote Swansea (Swansea Futures) which uses the strapline, 'It's a bay of life'. Moreover, one of the key objectives for the City Centre Strategy (launched two days ago) is to reunite the city centre with the Swansea Bay (often compared to the Bay of Naples!).

As you may know, we are just completing the TDAPs (Taught Degree Awarding Powers) procedure after which we will apply for a new university title. A strong runner in the latter stakes is 'Swansea Bay University', i.e. including a geographical feature in the title. Who else has done this? Southampton Solent, Nottingham Trent ...

*

There are some interestingly consistent themes here:

- the attraction to students (and possibly staff) of the seaside environment;
- the course-related opportunities – from science to the service economy;

- the sense of a special obligation to socioeconomic re-generation; and
- a kind of ironic satisfaction about the fun to be had at the seaside.

The concept of institutional reputation in colleges and universities is yet another example of HE 'exceptionalism'. It represents the point where internal self-image meets various relatively uncontrollable aspects of external evaluation. The former can be based on either strong or weak self-knowledge. The latter can be hijacked, not just by cultural prejudice, but also through the kind of spurious scientificity of league tables and the like.

The requirements seem to be for discipline and realism alongside ambition (the strictures regarding 'story-telling' come in here). The traps include on the one hand self-delusion, and on the other fatalism. It is at least as damaging to create and believe your own propaganda as to fuel and acquiesce in others. Reputation is rarely rapidly transformed, except occasionally downwards. But it is not static: it can build and it can decline.

Story-telling also validates the concept of the 'reputational re-servoir' set out in Watson and Maddison (2005: 142–4). It has an odd relationship with the practice of *praise* and *blame*. Here is an hy-pothesis: in institutions where the reservoir is full, blame is generally directed towards subordinates (see the submissions to the inquiry into the failure of the multi-million pound finance system, CAPSA, at Cambridge) (Finkelstein 2001); when empty, towards leaders (see the fate of the VC at Thames Valley University (TVU) as set out in the QAA report which led to his resignation) (Warner and Palfreyman 2003: 51–3).

We can all too easily confuse reputation and quality. There are reputations to be made – and defended – in the middle range. The inescapable fact is that reputation varies according to mission and activity, and not just in relation to performance.

To follow this up with an exercise, which of the league tables in Table 6.2 is most important to you as an institution? Among the 100 places represented here, 63 different institutions appear (in the pre-vious year there were 57).

Table 6.2 Ten 'top tens'

A Shanghai Jiao Tong Academic Ranking of World Universities (2008)

Cambridge (4)
Oxford (10)
UCL (22)
Imperial (27)
Manchester (40)
Edinburgh (55)
Bristol (61)
Sheffield (77)
KCL (81)
Nottingham (82)

Source: Institute of Higher Education, Shanghai Jiao Tong University (2007) (www.arwu.org/rank2008/en2008.htm)

B Times *League Table (2008)*

Oxford
Cambridge
Imperial College
LSE
St Andrews
Warwick
UCL
Durham
York
Bristol

Source: The Times Good University Guide (2009) (www.timesonline.co.uk)

C Research as a proportion of total FC grant (2006–7)

Imperial (28%)
UCL
Oxford
School of Pharmacy
St Andrews
Sussex
Sheffield
Bristol
Manchester
Southampton

Source: UUK (2008)

Table 6.2 continued

D   *Number of international (non-EU) students (2006–7)*

Manchester (6,390)
Nottingham
Warwick
London Metropolitan
Oxford
Northumbria
LSE
Cambridge
Birmingham
City

Source: UUK (2008)

E   *First destination survey – 'in employment' (2006–7)*

Royal College of Music (100%)
Royal Northern College of Music
Royal Veterinary College
School of Pharmacy
St George's Hospital Medical School
Canterbury Christ Church
Robert Gordon
Newman University College
Harper Adams University College
Nottingham Trent

Source: UUK (2008)

F   *National Student Survey (2008)*

Buckingham
Royal Academy of Music
Open
St Andrews
Courthauld Institute
Cambridge
Oxford
East Anglia
Birkbeck
Bishop Grosseteste

Source: THE 11 September 2008

Table 6.2 continued

G *Proportion of firsts and upper seconds (2006–7)*

Oxford (90%)
Liverpool Institute for Performing Arts
Cambridge
Conservatoire for Dance and Drama
St Andrews
Royal Academy of Music
Exeter
Edinburgh
Sussex
Guildhall School of Music & Drama

Source: UUK (2008)

H *Percentage of students from social groups 4–7 (2006–7)*

Harper Adams College (61%)
UHI Millennium Institute
St Mary's University College
Wolverhampton
Bradford
Birmingham College of Food, Tourism & Creative Studies
Sunderland
Middlesex
Ulster
Teesside

Source: UUK (2008)

I *The security index (2005–6)*

Birmingham College of Food, Tourism and Creative Studies
Bishop Grosseteste College
Liverpool Institute for the Creative Arts
Central School of Speech & Drama
Swansea Institute of HE
Bath Spa University
LSE
Royal Northern College of Music
University of Wales, Lampeter
Birmingham

Source: UUK (2008)

Table 6.2   continued

J   *Gay-friendly universities (according to* Diva *2005)*
Manchester Metropolitan
Brighton
University of London (!)
Birmingham
Lancaster
Leeds
Hull
Bradford
Durham
Edinburgh

Source: Guardian Online, 10 August 2005

To take the options in turn:

A   is the current obsession – as discussed in the last chapter.

B   is the domestic variant. It's a classic multiple factor table, and as a result it really tells you very little – other than about overall levels of resources.

C   is the table on which VCs think their reputations (and their re-muneration) rest (note that a small specialist institution – the School of Pharmacy – makes a first appearance).

D   represents one of our most intensively competitive markets (two large 'new' universities – London Metropolitan and Northumbria – join in).

E   is liked most by students and parents. The domination of the small and specialist is palpable here, but other anomalies include a free-standing medical school (St George's – the almost 100 per cent employment of other medical graduates is swallowed into larger university frameworks), as well as one large (very pro-fessionally orientated) 'new' university (Nottingham Trent).

F   has received a lot of attention during its first three years of life, but it is important to recognize that it tells us more about sub-jects than institutions. For example, art and design (where stu-dents are surveyed at the time of maximum personal stress – as they are preparing their final degree shows) receives notoriously low scores, with a corresponding effect on the institutional ranking where these loom large. Geologists are the happiest: perhaps it is the fieldwork (MacLeod 2008).

G   is at the time of writing the current moral panic. The race to inflate degree classes has been led by two types of institutions:

the prestigious (most of the Russell Group) and the precocious (some members of Guild HE).

H   is a standard measure of widening participation (it is important that these groups include – absurdly – the 'self-employed', among them farmers). Location is also highly influential – as in the University of the Highland and Islands.

I   is a consolidated measure of financial performance (and is a table that lay governors like). Strong performance here does not correlate with institutional status.

J   should not be dismissed out of hand (despite its journalistic flavour). There's a lot of work connecting gay lifestyles with creative communities, and (as evidenced by 'London' – very hard to pin down any longer as an identifiable singular 'university') it is really all about cities.

Leadership, governance and management ■

The most important issue about relating strategy, mission and reputation (in other words the conditions of the 'big story') is that of who decides, and how. At this point some definitions are in order. *Governance* is the exercise of stewardship of the institution as a whole, within a framework set by the institution's foundation and ongoing legal and/or constitutional status. This will also include ultimate responsibility for strategic direction. Governance is thus also about setting the conditions for and holding to account the leaders of the organization. *Leadership* is about setting the conditions for and then coordinating and motivating the performance of the institution. The third element of the trinity is *management*. This has a much more operational feel: it is about doing the right things and doing them well. In a university nearly everybody manages something and in turn is managed by others. Crudely, if governance is about stewardship, and leadership is about stretch, then management is about institutional strength.

Each university or college will have a 'supreme body' (normally a council, a governing board, or a board of trustees or overseers). This body (referred to below as the governing body) will be responsible for the assets of the institution as well as its strategic direction (often summarized in a phrase such as 'character and mission'). It will normally have a majority of 'lay' or 'independent' members.

The governing body itself will be constrained by the status of the institution in any particular jurisdiction: for example, the extent to which it is regulated by national or local laws, and the conditions under which it may receive public or private funds. Its formal status also entails auditing and reporting obligations (in the UK these are usefully summarized in both a guide and a code of practice produced by the Committee of University Chairmen) (CUC 2009). Some Governing bodies are also required to report to a wider group of parties with interests in the development of the university, such as a 'court' or a structured public meeting.

Nearly all universities will also have a supreme academic body (a senate, or academic board, referred to below simply as the academic board) to which either authority is formally delegated from the governing body, or in which authority is exercised as a founding right, over all academic matters. 'Academic governance' will generally cover matters such as the admission and discipline of students, the making of academic awards, and the conduct of teaching and research. Almost invariably the institution's primary function – of awarding degrees and other qualifications – will be subject to some form of regulation (either established by the founding authority or 'assured' through external accreditation or validation).

In most cases, internal members of the university (academic and support staff, as well as students) will have some representation on the governing body. In many cases the academic board will have the right to advise the governing body on key questions, such as resource allocation, some senior appointments, aspects of internal organization and strategic options. Some institutions also operate through joint or 'hybrid' committees bringing together lay members of the governing body and staff (and sometimes student) members, including nominees of the academic board. This phenomenon is described by the most authoritative British commentator, Michael Shattock, as 'shared governance', and is widely regarded as good practice (Shattock 2006: 58–80).

The leadership team has a special responsibility for oiling the wheels of shared governance, especially the head of the institution (president, rector, VC, principal or chief executive). He or she will generally be a member of the governing body and chair of the academic board (although this is rarely the case in Australia, where the chair of the academic board is usually elected rather than *ex officio*).

Over the past four years I have conducted a series of workshops for governing body chairs and chief executives of UK HEIs under the auspices of the LFHE. Putting together over 30 such 'pairs' in an environment away from their institutions and challenged to communicate with each other in both structured and unstructured ways, has thrown up a number of thorny issues. The big 'strategic' questions emerging include the following:

- understanding the performance of the institution compared with that of others in the sector;
- managing reputational risk;
- the boundaries between governance and management;
- governors' responsibility for senior appointments;
- succession;
- crisis management; and
- balancing institutional and public interests.

However some other, 'softer' dilemmas have also surfaced. These include:

- managing disagreement;
- dealing with a divided board;
- presenting the partnership to the board and the institution;
- offering genuine strategic choice and leadership;
- relative responsibilities for 'representing' the institution;
- relationships with multiple communities.

Further such issues are usefully covered in the report commissioned by the CUC from the Commonwealth Higher Education Management Services (CHEMS) Consulting, which also includes a comparison with other countries (the USA, Australia and New Zealand) as well as the corporate sector (CHEMS Consulting 2004).

Holding these contending forces together in a harsh and unforgiving world is ultimately a 'governance' or 'stewardship' role. Both the challenges and the outcomes (not least in contrast to the performance of the private sector) can be variously interpreted (see Schofield 2009). It is difficult for a high-performing board to maintain its level. To do so is mainly a question of self-renewal (continuing to appoint governors of the same or higher quality). But there is a process of entropy at work here. It is even harder for a less effective board to raise its game. First it has to know its own weaknesses, and the evidence suggests that this is hard. It goes, for example, against the grain of the occasionally aggressive overconfidence of some lay governors. Appointing governors who are better than you is a tough call.

There follows a classic contrast of 'witness statements' on the issues arising.

The first witness is the PA Consulting Group, in the latest of what has been a series of analytical (and predictive) statements about the condition of the UK sector:

The governance of higher education is complex, arcane and often antipathetic to modernisation and outward looking strategic change. Universities complain vociferously about the burdens imposed by the demands of public accountability and the vagaries of Ministerial policies. But in practice, these external constraints are at least matched by the sea anchors of internal procedures, committee structures and institutionalised conservatism that characterise most universities. Whether externally imposed or internally generated, the driver for most governance arrangements has been the maintenance of due processes – whether to assure that public finance requirements have been complied with, or to ensure that all interested parties have been duly consulted on proposals for change.

(PA Consulting 2008: 13)

This is a classic 'outside-in' view. Universities are self-regarding, procedurally hide-bound, risk-averse, over-anxious about 'process compliance' and oblivious to 'the results and outcomes achieved'. For an alternative, almost contemporaneous, 'inside-out' view see the following statement by Geoffrey Boulton and Colin Lucas on behalf of the League of European Research Universities (LERU). Their thesis is structured around the 'openness to contradiction that is part of the genius of universities':

A central dilemma for university governance is therefore how to retain the sense of ownership of the university enterprise by its members, which creates the setting for their creativity to range freely, whilst implementing the structural changes that are inevitably needed from time to time if a university is to remain a creative force for future generations ... Political boldness is also required. The freedom to enquire, to debate and to criticise and to speak truth to power, whether it be the power of government, of those who fund the university, or those who manage it, is central to the vitality of the university and its utility to society. It is crucial that rectors and university governing bodies understand this essential source of institutional strength, that they are steadfast in its support, strong in its defence and are not seduced by the fallacy of managerial primacy: that things that make management difficult need to be removed or reformed. An easily governed university is no university at all.

(Boulton and Lucas 2008: 15)

PA Consulting, of course, had the misfortune of going to press just before the failure of the western banking and financial services system demonstrated how seriously wrong things can go with a focus on 'results' rather than predetermined processes. Similarly, Boulton and Lucas might be accused of being ready to recognize universities' role in 'speaking truth to power' more readily than their prepared-ness to speak truth to themselves. However, as set out in Chapter 5, it is hard to speak against the longevity, the adaptability and the fun-damental ethical purpose of the university, despite its capacity (and propensity) to cry wolf and to fail from time to time to live up to its core mission and purposes. It is time to consider from where that mission and those purposes come.

The psychological contract

As set out in Chapter 4, despite the perception (and for some pur-poses the felt experience) of hierarchy, universities are very 'flat' in organization in some important respects. Almost all members have a right to be heard on institutional priorities. Their reputations rest – every day – on decisions made by individuals: the examiner marking the 'finals' paper; the admissions officer taking that difficult tele-phone call; the researcher deciding if a necessary adjustment to an investigative protocol has ethical implications; and so on.

In these circumstances, what is it that holds the internal com-munity together? Universities are (almost everywhere) voluntary corporations. What's the 'deal' (or to use the technical term, the 'psychological contract') when you join?

To be a full member of a university requires more than completing basic, obvious tasks. For traditional academics this has meant col-lective obligations: to assessment, to committee membership and to strategic scoping. There is a growing body of literature about what is now termed professional 'academic practice'.

Since the late twentieth century, and as described in Chapter 4, such practice has been recognized as no longer belonging exclusively to the ranks of the so-called 'faculty'. The teaching, research and service environments are increasingly recognized as being supported and developed by university members with a variety of expertise (e.g. finance, personnel, estates, libraries and ICT), each with their own spheres of professional competence, responsibility and recognition. The ways in which they work together are becoming increasingly purposive and complex.

At the heart of academic practice – and of academic citizenship – is the concept of membership, as set out in Chapter 4. This has several dimensions, ranging from status through legitimate expectations to inescapable obligations. As discussed in Chapter 3, as consumers, students have entitlements and expectations. Meanwhile, the force of Chapters 3 and 4 is that both students and staff (of all kinds) have responsibilities, along with all of their rights, within the community.

What exactly are these? As a contribution to the debate, I attempted in my *Managing Civic and Community Engagement* to scope out what the 10 commandments given to an HEI might be (Watson 2007b: 101–6; see also Watson 2007a). The resulting 'Hippocratic Oath' is reprised below, along with some second thoughts.

1 *Strive to tell the truth.* 'Academic freedom', in the sense of following difficult ideas wherever they may lead, is possibly the fundamental 'academic' value.

2 *Take care in establishing the truth.* Adherence to scientific method is critical here (as in the use of evidence, and the 'falsifiability' principle), but so too is the concept of social scientific 'warrant' and the search for 'authenticity' in the humanities and arts. There's a particular type of academic bad faith, which moves too quickly to rhetoric and persuasion in advance of the secure establishment of the grounds for conviction. As the physicist Richard Feynman says: in science, whenever you have a good idea, your first obligation is to think about everything that might be wrong with it. For me this is a truth that applies beyond science. Feynman apparently agreed. He apologized to the director of the American Museum of Natural History about having called social science 'pseudoscientific', going on to praise contributions in 'anthropology, history, archaeology, etc., which I admire' (Feynman 2005: 360). He also became engaged in a notorious tenure case at CalTech (of Jenijoy Labelle, who became the university's first female professor), declaring that colleagues in her subject (English) 'have done a great deal to us and our students to make this place livable and human, as the Department of Humanities is meant to' (2005: 301).

3 *Be fair.* This is about equality of opportunity, non-discrimination and perhaps even affirmative action. Along with 'freedom' in the academic value system goes 'respect for persons'. High morale seems to be deeply dependent upon this.

4 *Always be ready to explain.* Academic freedom is a 'first amendment' and not a 'fifth amendment' right; it is about freedom of speech and not about protection from self-incrimination (Watson 2000: 85–7). It does not absolve any member of the academic community from the obligation to explain his or her actions, and as far as possible their consequences. Accountability is inescapable, and should not be unreasonably resisted.

5 *Do no harm.* This is where the assessment of consequences cashes

out (and presents the academy's nearest equivalent to the Hippocratic Oath, to strive 'not to harm but to help'). It is about non-exploitation, either of human subjects or of the environment. It underpins other notions like 'progressive engagement' (when decisions are taken according to whether they will move the organization towards or away from substantial goals – if only in small steps). It helps with really wicked issues like the use of animals in medical experiments (as in the 'three Rs' injunction of 'replacement, reduction and refinement', originally formulated as long ago as 1954) (Zurlo *et al.* 1996).

6   *Keep your promises.* Universities and colleges are involved in a variety of contracts and partnerships. Their record is good: on large-scale projects – on which millions of pounds rest – the examples of the university partner walking away from a done deal are very rare. Meanwhile, the commercial partner can (and often does) withdraw, citing changes in strategy, the business cycle or even changes in management. As indicated in Chapter One, the 'credit crunch' brings about extra pressure here: not least through the pressure on arrangements like the Private Finance Initiative, in which long-term, risk-transference agreements are struck with business partners. Such, 'business' excuses for retreating from or unreasonably seeking to re-negotiate agreements are much less acceptable in an academic context.

7   *Respect your colleagues, your students and especially your opponents.* Working in an academic community means listening as well as speaking, seeking always to understand the other point of view, and ensuring that rational discourse is not derailed by prejudice, by egotism or by bullying of any kind. As argued in Chapter 4, civility in academic life is functional as well as more pleasant.

The last point is where speech codes and protocols come in, as well as their related sanctions, sometimes with unintended effects. There is a large question about whether these are aimed at mandating behaviour or belief. In other words, people can maintain a satisfactory relationship with the community even when they share neither its values nor its conclusions, provided that they are prepared to behave *as if* they do. As Elizabeth I is reputed to have said to Philip of Spain, 'I have no desire to make windows into men's souls'.

Helping to probe some of these dilemmas, we now have a rather weak, but nonetheless, worked example. In June 2005 the American Council of Education (ACE) produced a 'Statement on Academic Rights and Responsibilities' in response to the energetic critic of academic bias on campus, David Horowitz (inspirer and maintainer of classroom surveillance websites and author of *The Professors: The*

101 Most Dangerous Academics in America) (Smith *et al.* 2008: 66, 94–8). What I think this primarily shows is (as in Smith *et al.*'s authoritative study of the campus bias controversy) the collusive interest of both sides in fudging the issue. The ACE document itself is naturally limited; it was, of course, born of the kind of compromise that involves both sides backing down: they knew he would not go away; Horowitz knew he would lose conservative support if it looked like he was turning government into the 'school board for America'.

The ACE Statement also gets things the wrong way round. Its goal is a rather weasely concept of 'intellectual pluralism' (which it puts before 'academic freedom'). It also proposes remedies ('any member of a campus community who believes he or she has been treated unfairly on academic matters must have access to a clear institutional process by which his or her grievance can be addressed') before it incorporates any sense of mission. When the latter comes it is introduced in terms of the classic disclaimer with which the American Association of University Professors (AAUP) structured its groundbreaking definition of academic freedom in 1915: academics should not comment on matters apparently outside of their fields.

> The validity of academic ideas, theories, arguments and views should be measured against the intellectual standards of relevant academic and professional disciplines. Application of these intellectual standards does not mean that all ideas have equal merit. The responsibility to judge the merits of competing academic ideas rests with colleges and universities and is determined by reference to the standards of the academic profession as established by the community of scholars at each institution.
>
> (Smith *et al.* 2008: 237)

8   *Sustain the community.* All of the values so far expressed are deeply communal. Obligations that arise are not just to the subject or professional community, or even to the institution in which you might be working at any one time, but (as suggested in Chapter 5) to the family of institutions that make up the university sector, nationally and internationally.

9   *Guard your treasure.* University and college communities, and those responsible for leading and managing them, are in the traditional sense 'stewards' of real and virtual assets (including libraries, galleries, collections and buildings), and of the capacity to continue to operate responsibly and effectively.

10 *Never be satisfied.* Perhaps this is the academic equivalent of the golden rule. Academic communities understood the principles of

'continuous improvement' long before they were adopted by 'management' literature. They also understand its merciless and asymptotic nature. The academic project will never be complete or perfect.

In other words, my claim is that there exist value domains which are special to HE, and which in wider contexts constitute HE's contributions to civil society in all of its endeavours. One domain is clearly about how knowledge is effectively and responsibly created, tested and used. Another is about how people responsibly interact with each other (including what they take from the university when they move outside it). And a third is about the institutional presence of universities and colleges in a wider society; in other words, about their civic and community responsibilities.

An important consideration is how far these injunctions are culturally specific. Are they inescapably 'nested' in a western, perhaps even a European, view of the context and of the possibilities of a university culture? In *Managing Civic and Community Engagement* I argued not – except in one vital respect. They will not work where the institution's primary purpose is dogmatic instruction, not least from a doctrinal point of view. At least since the European Enlightenment, systematic reference to (and validation by) revealed religion will undermine both the universally agreed mode of inquiry (of knowledge creation, testing and use) and the intended destination (which for this value system needs always to be provisional) (Watson 2007b: 106).

At the school level, Lynne Davies (introduced in Chapter 3) comes to a very similar conclusion. 'Faith' will not do the job we need done for inclusive inquiry, and science is our only hope of incorporating pluralism without relativizing truth. She argues strongly for a curriculum and a pedagogy structured around rights and a secular morality:

As well as cutting out the middle man, the brilliant thing about a rights base is that it also circumvents the problem of 'tolerance'. I can accept your right to believe in a culture or religion without having to accept the religion itself. As argued earlier, belief systems by definition cannot be equal or equally valid; but our right to believe in what we want, as long as this does not cause harm to others, is – and must be – equally distributed. Rights and responsibilities together deny the possibility of indoctrination and imposition of beliefs.

(Davies 2008: 162–3)

However, despite my common cause with Davies, I don't think I have fully solved the issue of faith-based institutional settings. What is and is not up for grabs in these? How much has to be open to question for these institutions to belong to today's HE family? An institution that is a comfortable and supportive place for members of a faith community to live and work together is one thing; for the precepts of that faith to limit inquiry is another. And this may not be just about religious creeds; there are equally contentious issues around complementary medicine and alternative therapies. Many scholars are trying to establish appropriate boundaries. As Mona Sidiqqui, professor of Islamic studies and public understanding at the University of Glasgow suggests, 'all that is needed … is a more relaxed approach towards faith within secular universities' (Fearn 2009). It is interesting that for Smith *et al.* (conscious of the large number of faith-based institutions in the USA), institutional mission-specificity overrides what I would regard as the essential conditions of commandments 1, 2 and 4:

> Government's recognition and respect for the independence of colleges and universities is essential for academic and intellectual excellence. Because colleges and universities have great discretion over academic affairs, they have a particular obligation to ensure that academic freedom is protected for all members of the academic community and that academic missions are based on intellectual standards consistent with the mission of each institution.
>
> (Smith *et al.* 2008: 237)

Absent these constraining conditions (which I am still reluctant to accept), and the commandments seem to work. They include the core role of HE (what is genuinely 'higher' about it) as a 'conversation' between more and less experienced learners (remember Ed Husain from Chapter 3). There is also the vital principle of mutual respect: between staff and student members of the university; between institutions; between national systems; and between universities and their communities.

It is also possibly true that in some ways universities are less exceptional than they used to be. It would be deeply ironic if university boards (following PA Consulting) began to operate like banks just as banks decide to operate like universities. Meanwhile, we have the phenomenon of an increasing number of successful 'university-like businesses'.

For one thing, they take learning and teaching seriously. Here's a famous literary example, from our regular academic *raisonneur*, David

Lodge. Robyn Penrose, the young academic 'twinned' with the businessman Vic Wilcox in *Nice Work*, comes to see that – just like her – he is a teacher:

> Pringles was definitely a business dealing in real commodities and running it was not in the least like doing literary theory, but it did strike Robyn sometimes that Vic Wilcox stood to his subordinates in the relation of teacher to pupils … she could see that he was trying to *teach* the other men and persuade them to look at the factory's operations in a new way. He would have been surprised to be told it, but he used the Socratic method: he prompted the other directors and the middle managers and even the foremen to identify the problems themselves and to reach by their own reasoning the solutions he had already determined upon. It was so deftly done that she had to temper her admiration by reminding herself that it was all directed by the profit motive …
>
> (Lodge 1988: 758)

Here is a more hard-nosed witness: Gary Hamel from the London School of Business: 'anyone who has ever run a university, a film studio, or an open source software project will tell you that getting the most out of people seldom means managing them more, and usually means managing them less' (Hamel 2007: 60).

Hamel goes on to give some case studies of 'university-like businesses':

- Whole Foods approach to management twines democracy with discipline, trust with accountability and community with fierce internal competition (p. 72).
- [W.L.] Gore wins big by not betting big, but betting often and staying at the table long enough to collect its winnings (p. 95).
- Like an elite engineering school, Google's management model is built around small work units, lots of experimentation, vigorous peer feedback, and a mission to improve the world (p. 107). As is true in academic life or on the Web, control at Google is more peer-to-peer than manager to minion (p. 111).
- Torvalds [Linux] understands that in a community of peers, people bow to competence, commitment, and foresight, rather than power' (p. 207). Like professors vying to get published in prestigious journals, coders hanker for the peer recognition that comes from making a visible contribution … The lesson: a successful opt-in system is one that allows contributors to take their 'psychic income' in a variety of currencies (p. 209).

Even big pharma – perhaps in response to the credit crunch – seems to be joining in. In early 2009 the new chief executive of GlaxoSmithKline, Andrew Whitty, announced not only cuts in drug prices for developing countries and re-investment of profits in their health care systems but also an open 'patent pool' for intellectual property relating to neglected diseases and an invitation to other companies to 'join the hunt for tropical disease treatments' (Boseley 2009). Among his rewards was an 'in praise of' editorial in *The Guardian* (14 February 2009) for what catching up with the 'emerging lesson of open source software', even if it is acknowledged that 'as always in ethical business, there is an element of enlightened self-interest'.

A grown-up culture

So how do we operate at our best? Again, as I have argued elsewhere, the story of universities as institutions – and of the project nobly called HE – is a story of continuity and change: of looking backwards and looking forwards (Watson 2007b: 9, 85–6).

Today what we are experiencing is a flurry of interest in institutions as (in the philosopher Samuel Scheffler's phrase) 'infra-structures of responsibility'. In an important paper in the *Journal of Applied Philosophy* (Williams 2006), Garrath Williams seeks to establish 'the moral task of institutions' in three domains: defining and inculcating practical morality; allocating responsibility, initiative and power; and providing recognition and identity for actors. He also speculates about why the grand liberal tradition of social theory has found institutions difficult: because of what he calls their 'ideational bias' (focusing on belief more than on action); because of their optimism about overcoming 'normative disagreement'; because of their legalism; and because of the tradition's obsession with corrupt institutions.

Williams' analysis captures some important ways in which universities have always operated at their best. The HE project incorporates a profound sense of stewardship, and of handing on of key commitments and values; but it also incorporates a permanent undertow of unfinished business, of more and new things to do. In the process, colleges and universities carry considerable moral freight: they know that they count.

So, universities and colleges are very special institutions in modern society. Contrary to some popular beliefs they have always been very practical and responsive places: creating and establishing new knowledge and teaching new skills to cope with changing circumstances. In other words, perhaps more than any other enduring institution in our history, they have proved capable of reinventing themselves to meet new demands. Meanwhile, while each university has its distinctive but changing history, another part of the university enterprise has always remained the same. We have in our business what Einstein called a 'cosmological constant'. There has always been an independent, deeply ethical part of our work that is critical and concerned about enduring values: values such as scientific honesty, openness to new and uncomfortable ideas, tolerance, as well as human emancipation. The 'trinity' of governance, leadership and management has special responsibilities here.

With some honourable (mostly American) exceptions, systematic scholarly work on leadership in HE was largely absent from the literature until relatively late in the twentieth century. What did exist – and were occasionally useful or inspiring – were wry gentlemanly reflections by leaders towards or at the end of their careers on what seemed to have worked (at least for them; I am aware of the irony of this observation). At the same time the railway/airport bookstands were groaning under the weight of faddish works claiming to offer miracle applications of theory (usually psychological) to the general problems of leadership in corporate life.

In the last two decades this has all changed. HEIs are seen as serious (social) businesses to be managed; the expectations of performance (and of accountability) are high; and – oddly, given the objectively strong record of universities and colleges in meeting new challenges and avoiding disaster – there is a public and political perception of leadership deficit, especially in the UK. There have, of course, been near misses (Cardiff's budget, Lancaster's bond, TVU's stand-off with QAA, Glasgow Caledonian's Malaysian adventures, and Cambridge's CAPSA melt-down), but British HE still awaits its Millennium Dome or Terminal 5 moment. Meanwhile, as suggested by Hamel, it may be true that HE has a lesson or two to teach twenty-first century, knowledge-intensive businesses.

As for the characteristics and conditions of this ideal, grown-up culture, I suggest that they include at least the following:

- emotionally intelligent interactions, at all levels of the institution;
- pragmatically responsible decision-making (e.g. in not defending the indefensible);
- a commitment to the corporate self-knowledge that comes from sound self-study (or institutional research);
- regular practice of self-care by all groups in the organization (as the analyst Gerhard Wilke [2000: 4] suggests, 'we often lead a split

role; we own all of our skills in the role of therapist but forbid ourselves to use them in the role of employee').

Adrian Furnham (2004: 106) has a special set of strictures on the question of morale and perceived fairness:

> Morale, like commitment endures. But it can be broken and, if so, is not easy to repair. Morale is also linked to the concept of fairness. Nothing lowers morale more than nepotism, favouritism or corruption. People have a strong need to feel equitably dealt with: they need to feel that effort and output will be fairly rewarded.

Equally important are the conditions of self-care. One of the main successes of the happiness industry is the establishment of what has been called the 'project of the self'. Part of this is about the 'task of keeping healthy' (Beck and Beck-Gernsheim 2002: 140). Johanna Wyn has analysed in great detail how this affects the prospects of the members of Generations X, Y and Z (Wyn 2008). Self-care is an essential (but rarely surfaced) implication of both the 'psychological contract' within HE (as in my Hippocratic Oath above) and the 'grown-up culture'. The study referred to at the head of this chapter refers to particular vulnerabilities, in:

> male staff, older staff, longer serving staff, full-time staff, staff reporting working more than 50 hours a week; and staff reporting more sickness absence. Those reporting working more than 50 hours in a typical working week (approximately 15% of HEI staff) reported higher stress, particularly related to demands, and this effect was very much accentuated for those working more than 60 hours. This group also reported a poorer work-life balance, more conflict and lower support than those working fewer hours.
>
> (Auty 2008; see also www.qowl.co.uk)

When the project of the self meets corporate commitment to change the result can be dangerous to both.

In universities the zone of self-managed activity is relatively wide and relatively deep. Day-to-day scrutiny and reporting on core and routine activity is minimal. This is especially the case in terms of academic work (teaching and research) where the traditional accusation of a 'secret garden' is nothing like as relevant as it used to be, but still has some residual force. I recall one of my former bosses telling external members of the board of governors that some of them might find it difficult to believe, but 'the only way to know if academics are on strike is to ask them'. This type of freedom is liberating, but it can also be frightening.

The trajectory of quality assessment of teaching in England is illuminating here, as a kind of test case of how ideological capture of core functions can undermine morale.

One of the most distinctive features of the development of the UK system of HE has been its willingness to take academic responsibility for its own enlargement. The UK system is admired around the world for its commitment to systematic peer review. So it is deeply ironic that at home the 'quality wars' have threatened to tear the sector apart. If you take the long historical view, the 'collaborative' gene was there from the start, for example through London external degrees and the system of 'validating universities' (notably the Victoria University of Manchester). External members of university college committees played their part in the late nineteenth and early twentieth centuries, before the two major phases of late twentieth-century expansion. These were overseen, in turn, by 'academic advisory committees' for the post-Robbins foundations and the CNAA for what was termed 'public sector higher education'. All this sat alongside 'academic' contributions to other 'quality assurance' agencies, including both the accrediting and 'recognition' role of professional and statutory bodies (PSBs) and the more direct 'inspection' role of the state (Her Majesty's Inspectorate [HMI] and latterly the Office for Standards in Education [Ofsted]). But perhaps the most potent symbol is that of the 'external examiner', a figure of immense moral importance, significantly envied in other systems.

Following the Conservative legislation of 1988 and 1992, some of these functions were indeed bureaucratized, and the sector tried – late in the day – to take pre-emptive action against the encroachment of the state. But the paradox was that, as the world beat a path to the UK door to learn about how to do some of these things, a series of 'popular revolts' at home did their best to do away with them, and in so far as they were successful they undermined the self-regulating, collegial instincts of the sector as a whole (Watson 2006).

Against this background of loose self-management there are, of course, certain lines in the sand: deadlines, contractual commitments, reporting obligations, expectations of timely response to inquiries, and so on. Responsibility for these often rests with quite junior officers, who may have to manage both their own performance and that of more senior (and less constrained) colleagues in order to deliver. It is revealing to identify who are the 'officers of last resort' for key university functions: the members of staff for whom a deadline is genuinely a deadline. It is then interesting to see where personal 'stress' is claimed, discovered and/or recognized by support systems (Fisher 1994). The correlation is sometimes counter-intuitive.

Self-care also sits in a context of 'group' responsibilities of various kinds: to a local team, a department or a disciplinary or professional 'tribe', or increasingly to temporary or semi-permanent project teams (Celia Whitchurch's home for 'third-space' professionals) (Whitchurch 2008b). Academic 'tribes' were famously examined by Tony Becher in his classic work of 1989. They still resound powerfully in discussions of university morale. As I discussed the topic of this book with academics (and reflected on the '100 voices') the strength of disciplinary identity, loyalty and solidarity rang through. There was also a sense of the vulnerability of these values, and in some cases, their loss. It is interesting to note that in the second edition (2001), Becher and his co-author Paul Trowler felt obliged to put up some warning signs:

> Meanwhile changes to the higher education system, the internal character of universities and to the very meaning of higher education have resulted in a highly differentiated, more permeable, system in which close engagement with the disciplinary knowledge core through research is only one activity among very many. For a good proportion of academics it is not a significant aspect of their world at all ... The emphasis on the epistemological in social construction has thus been squeezed from two directions: by real world changes and by theoretical shifts. Like academics themselves, whose claims to exceptionalism no longer find a sympathetic audience in the contemporary context of postmodern delegitimation, the 'special' significance of disciplinary knowledge has been diminished. It has not disappeared though; it remains a significant factor to be taken into account in attempting to understand the academic profession, albeit one which needs to be understood in a slightly different way than was once the case.
>
> (Becher and Trowler 2001: xii–xiv)

This recognition of 'mode 2' conditions of work further enhances the injunctions of self-care. It is no accident that Paul Gray and David Drew's witty guide to 'success in your academic career' culminates in a series of injunctions to 'stay healthy' (Gray and Drew 2008: 139–45). What they say should apply to all members of staff. At all levels and across all functions, the university shows up a peculiar combination of expectations of self-management, the need for considerable self-confidence, and the desirability of emotional intelligence.

Managing morale is thus ultimately about achieving various sorts of balance: between continuity and change; between challenge and reassurance; between protection and independence; between pressure and relief; and between ambition and humility. It can be inculcated through example, but that is not enough. Leadership has to be matched with effective governance and management to make the mission stick.

CODA

∎

In this final section I collect some (even more) personal reflections on the role of leadership in creating an appropriate climate for the university mission to flourish. What is a happy enough university? How do those in leadership roles take responsibility for helping it to be so? What about their personal responsibilities for self-care?

The quantum of happiness

∎

One of Ian Fleming's best pieces of writing is a short story called 'Quantum of Solace'. It has nothing at all to do with the 2008 film of the same name. It concerns the smallest unit of human compassion two people can share, below which a relationship becomes impossible (Fleming 1962: 84–108). As the governor of Bermuda explains to James Bond about a tortured relationship:

> They can survive almost anything as long as some kind of basic humanity exists between the two people. When all kindness is gone, when one person obviously and sincerely doesn't care if the other is alive or dead then it's just no good. That particular insult to the ego – worse to the instinct of self-preservation – can never be forgiven.
>
> (p. 100)

This is rather like what happens when a member of the university gives up on the institution, or the institution's representatives do the same in return. John Armstrong, in his *Conditions of Love*, has probed the relationship between love and hate in philosophical terms. Not only is the relationship between the two profoundly ambivalent, but: 'The secondary worry – the one which really knocks us off our course – is the panicky voice which shouts out: I thought I loved this person but now I'm miserable, it's all over, our love is finished. This is like the despair that prevents people from writing' (Armstrong 2005: 133).

Is there a 'quantum of happiness' without which universities cannot survive as successful communities? In Weiner's account of Bhutan's concept of gross national happiness (GNH), there is a similar notion. One of its architects explains how it is constructed not around a striving for nirvana, but more around self-knowledge, 'knowing your limitations, knowing how much is enough' (Weiner 2008: 106).

Another promising metaphor is around temperature. We may have our own special version of the Gaia thesis at work in HEIs. Too low an institutional temperature and there will be dull, complacent systems maintenance. Too high, and hysteria will take over. Guy Browning puts the point even more straightforwardly in his *Guardian* column (2008):

> Restless discontent is often held up as the great wellspring of personal and artistic progress. This is the ants-in-the-pants theory of progress and works well if you think progress consists of substituting one state of unhappiness with another. That said, contentment can be dangerously close to the squishy sofas of smugness and complacency. It's worth remembering your lot can quite easily be an epic struggle against overwhelming odds, but, even if it is, you can still be content with it.
>
> (Browning 2008)

In an organization like a university or college, where the fundamental injunction is never to be satisfied, this final paradox can make sense. What I have been trying to address through the question of morale is the sense of efficacy, of purposive engagement, of satisfaction, and of feeling valued, a member of the HE community. This is (as Furnham says in the essay quoted at the beginning) a property of both individuals and groups. In the HE setting, I think it is especially about groups, and about membership groups across a spectrum: from the immediate team to those for whom a sense of responsibility is felt, however remote the connection (e.g. from my course team, or department, to all specialists in the same subject, and to all similar employees across the sector).

Digression 11: Marcus Aurelius and the power of the adage

Thinking hard about morale also leads to an understanding of an essential leadership truth (endlessly recycled since Marcus Aurelius) that people who feel good about themselves do better work. They will also feel better if the sense of self-direction is high. In this context, for senior managers, one of the most celebrated *Meditations* rings with particular force: 'treat with respect the power you have to form an opinion'.

The power of this kind of thinking came to me in email correspondence with Paul Ramsden (then of the University of Sydney, now chief executive of the Higher Education Academy), who has researched the issue of academic leadership (an oxymoronic concept for many within the academy) as intensively as anyone I know. In the course of an exchange about my foreword to the second edition of his best-seller *Learning to Teach in Higher Education* (Ramsden 2003), I shared with Paul some of the 'adages' I have developed about senior management in universities (these can be found in Watson 2003). Paul came back with some of his own, and this arresting coda:

> My personal experience of top academic and institutional leadership is that the most serious faults are arrogance, intimidation, mistrust, timidity in delegation, and the curious phenomenon of oscillation between no clear direction and micro-management. These weaknesses apparently sit comfortably alongside otherwise admirable features such as efficiency, hard work and decisiveness and they set a ceiling on their holders' effectiveness as leaders and managers. They seem to be part of a syndrome of insecurity and lack of faith in other people. I fear that they will not be touched by any leadership programme – but I do hope I am wrong!

Paul went on:

> Re. leadership development, I think that the useful experiences are those in which the older and wiser and very successful describe key moments in their careers, some of which are examples of triumph over adversity and others of which are examples of learning from mistakes.

One upshot was our view that perhaps the field might benefit from a Marcus Aurelius-Alain de Botton style volume aimed at the VC's holiday book bag (an early version of the welcome pack described in Digression 7).

Most of the more celebrated adages are versions of the golden mean, or the search for equilibrium. There is 'Gaia' (above) – about temperature. There is the notion of some members of the community adding value and others subtracting it. And then there is the old baseball adage that a successful team is rarely as good as it seems and an unsuccessful one rarely as bad (in Michael Lewis' *Moneyball* the statistical proof for this theorem is evinced – providing another argument for self-study [see Lewis 2004: 129–37; E. Smith 2008: 89–93]). Geoffrey Howe said something very similar about politics.

Learning from good and bad practice ▪

What is and should be the response of university management to the analysis here? In general, today's HE managers are interested not so much in bland injunctions to good practice as in detailed evisceration of bad practice ('there but for the grace of God go I').

Management concepts have market values. *Management Today* notoriously scores them out of 10 and assesses whether they are holding, rising or falling. At the time of writing, 'best practice' is probably poised for a fall, and management teams are advised to sell. Partly this is because of conceptual incoherence: when 'best practice' becomes 'rolled out' (and becomes 'common' or 'good' practice) it can no longer be called best. (This is a version of Garrison Keillor's *Lake Wobegon*, where all of the children are above average). It is partly because (if they are honest) serious managers do not read the bland so-called 'good practice' guides. They think that the material is boring, and that they know it all already. So the guides get marked up for some subordinate's attention, or (more frequently) filed under the desk. They also have a suspicion that many of the sector-wide groups regularly making use of this genre (the funding councils, the QAA, LFHE, CUC and so on) are simply laying off their own responsibilities (the government says to the funding councils, 'deal with risk' or 'confront extremism', and the only recourse is to identify another reporting line for the institutions).

What really turns senior managers on is when the wheels come off, and they can read about other people's bad practice-related disasters. Some of these were rehearsed at the end of Chapter 6. However, what the litany there did not include is the record of what Peter Scott calls near misses or 'near-crises' (Warner and Palfreyman 2003: 169). He goes on to identify four potential sources of institutional crisis: 'underlying weakness of the institution', 'ineffective management systems', 'a lack of clarity about strategic direction' and 'people and personalities' (he focuses, as I have for much of this book, on governance and leadership) (Warner and Palfreyman 2003: 169–73). Each of these pathologies can fester under the surface and undermine positive morale, and it takes positive personal attitudes and action to improve the situation. University members need to learn from their own as well as others' mistakes. Individuals have to have the courage to cut into the cycles of rationalization and group-think that the culture can encourage and recognize the value of early intervention in bad situations. They also have to apply the same standards of respect for evidence and for others' opinions that they employ in their scholarly and professional work. Assertion does not make it so.

Final digression: the third envelope

There is a hoary old joke, much beloved of retiring principals and head teachers. On taking office the new incumbent is handed three numbered envelopes by his or her predecessor and told to open them in sequence in response to crises. The first crisis reveals a note reading 'blame the previous administration'. The second advises 'say it's too early to judge'. The message in the third is brutal: 'prepare three envelopes'.

I offered the third envelope to my successor in September 2005, after an extremely happy (but not crisis-free) spell of 15 years as the head of Brighton Polytechnic and then the University of Brighton.

I argued then (as I have here, especially in Chapter 6) that universities are very peculiar places. They are professionally argumentative communities, with very flat structures. More or less everybody is authorized to have an opinion about everything. Meanwhile, universities have their own laws. Here are a few of them.

The laws of academic life

- Issues generate heat in inverse proportion to their importance (think of car-parking).
- Academics grow in confidence the further away they are from their true fields of expertise (what you really know about is provisional and ambiguous, what other people do is clear-cut and usually wrong).

- You should never go to a school or department for anything which is in its title (which university consults its architecture department on the estate, or – heaven forbid – its business school on the budget?).
- The first thing a committee member says is the exact opposite of what she or he means ('I'd like to agree with everything the VC has just said, but ... ; or 'with respect' ... ; or even 'briefly').
- Courtesy is a one-way street (social-academic language is full of hyperbole, and one result is the confusion of rudeness – or even cruelty – with forthrightness; however, if a manager responds in kind, it's a federal case).
- On email nobody ever has the last word.
- Somebody always does it better elsewhere (because they are better supported).
- Feedback only counts if I agree with it.
- The temptation to say 'I told you so' is irresistible.
- Finally, there is never enough money, but there used to be.

And so, the message in my third envelope goes something like this (these are the lessons I think I've learned – sometimes painfully).

The third envelope

- When you don't know how to take the big steps, take the most sensible next little step.
- Everyone deserves a second chance (including yourself).
- Trust your instincts, but be prepared to revise them in the light of experience.
- There is no difficult letter which cannot be improved by eight hours sleep.
- Look at all of your post.
- Draft your emails.
- Try to learn people's names.
- Don't pretend to know when you don't (you will always be found out).
- Say thank you, even (especially?) when you don't mean it.
- Your most important (perhaps your only) tool for change is creative temporary cross-subsidy.

The tenth secret is the most important. This is a radically non-heroic proposition, but it works. To make it work you need to have (or to create) a sense of corporate commitment that taps into both altruism and self-interest. You also need financial discipline, in order to create the necessary margins.

What have I tried to say in this book? Universities are peculiar places, especially in the ways in which people relate to each other. They are both insulated from and implicated in the ongoing and the transient concerns of a wider community (whose interest in their affairs is growing, not receding). Corporately and collectively, they can behave well or badly on a number of levels, as can the individuals within them. At their best they can achieve remarkable things; at their worst they can be petty, corrosive, even dangerous. There is no formula that will automatically spring benign or productive outcomes. Indeed there is potential hubris in books with titles like Managing Successful Universities. *However, they will do better – in general – the greater the degree of corporate self-knowledge they are able to achieve; including perhaps from time to time the ability to laugh at themselves. In* The Question of Morale *I have tried to sketch the contours of such self-knowledge, in an appropriately respectful and provisional way.*

LIST OF WEBSITES

(all last accessed on 31 March 2009)

Cambridge Well-Being Institute: www.cambridgewellbeing.org/
Centre for Effective Dispute Resolution: www.cedr.co.uk/
Chartered Management Institute: www.managers.org.uk/
Chronicle of Higher Education: www.chronicle.com/
Civil Mediation Council: www.civilmediation.org/
Department for Innovation, Universities and Science: www.dius.gov.uk/
Higher Education Academy: www.heacademy.ac.uk/
Higher Education Funding Council for England: www.hefce.ac.uk
Inquiry into the Future for Lifelong Learning: www.niace.org.uk/lifelong
    learninginquiry/
Intercollegiate Studies Institute: www.isi.org/
National Accounts of Wellbeing (New Economics Foundation):
    www.nationalaccountsofwellbeing.org/
Office of the Independent Adjudicator: www.oiahe.org.uk/
Oxford Centre for Higher Education Policy Studies: http://oxcheps.new.ox.
    ac.uk/
Quality Assurance Agency for Higher Education: www.qaa.ac.uk
Society for Research into Higher Education: www.srhe.ac.uk
Teaching and Learning Research Programme: www.tlrp.org/
Times Higher Education: www.timeshighereducation.co.uk/
Unison: www.unison.org.uk/
Universities and Colleges Employers' Association: www.ucea.edu/
Universities and Colleges Union: www.ucu.org.uk/
Universities UK: www.universitiesuk.ac.uk/

REFERENCES

Acheson, N. (2007) Diary, *London Review of Books*, 5 April: 38–9.

Acocella, J. (2008) The child trap: the rise of overparenting, *The New Yorker*, 17 November: 100–5.

Adams, J. (2008) *Hallelujah Junction: Composing an American Life*. London: Faber & Faber.

Ahier, J., Beck, J. and Moore, R. (2002) *Graduate Citizens? Issues of citizenship and Higher Education*. London: Routledge Falmer.

Alderman, G. (2009) Can't think, won't think, *Times Higher Education*, 5 March: 7.

Allen, D. (2008) University leaders: keeping the hopper full, paper presented at the Leadership in HE Symposium, St George's House, Windsor, 31 March – 1 April), mimeo.

Anonymous (2006) *A Campus Conspiracy*. Exeter: Impress Books.

Armstrong, J. (2003) *Conditions of Love: The Philosophy of Intimacy*. London: Penguin.

Ashby, E. (1958) *Technology and the Academics*. London: Macmillan.

Aspden, P. (2007) How to be a middle-aged man, *Financial Times*, 11 August.

Atwood, M. (2008) *Payback: Debt and the Shadow Side of Wealth*. London: Bloomsbury.

Auty, C. (2008) Managing stress in the HE workplace, AUA *Newslink*, 59(1).

Bacon, E. (2009) Do professional managers have a profession? The specialist/generic distinction amongst higher education professional staff, *Perspectives: Policy and Practice in UK Higher Education* 13(1): 10–15.

Baggini, J. (2008) *Complaint: From Minor Moans to Principled Protest*. London: Profile.

Banajai, S. (2008) The trouble with civic: a snapshot of young people's civic and political engagements in twenty-first-century democracies, *Journal of Youth Studies*, 11(5): 543–60.

Barmania, N. (2009) This Muslim life, *The Guardian*, 6 February: 17.

Barnett, R. (2007) *A Will to Learn: Being a Student in an Age of Uncertainty*. Maidenhead: Open University Press.

Barrett, S. (2008) This muddy site is fan's paradise, *Brighton & Hove Argus*, 18 December: 14–15.

Baty, P. and Wainwright, T. (2005) Lecture's off. I want my bus fare refunded, *Times Higher Education*, 19 August.

Bauman, Z. (2008) *The Art of Life*. Cambridge: Polity.

BBC News Online (2007) UK is accused of failing children, 6 September.

BBC News Online (2008a) Misery: the secret to happiness, 2 January.

BBC News Online (2008b) Students tell of fees resentment,11 April.

BBC News Online (2009) Colleges face £170m projects loss, 20 March.

Becher, T. and Trowler, P. (2001) *Academic Tribes and Territories*, 2nd edn. Buckingham: SRHE and Open University Press.

Beck, U. and Beck-Gernsheim, E. (2002) *Individualization: Institutionalized Individualism and its Social and Political Consequences*. London: Sage.

Beddington, J., Cooper, C., Field, J., Goswami, U., Huppert, F., Jenkins, R., Jones, H., Kirkwood, T., Sahakian, B. and Thomas, S. (2008) The mental wealth of nations, *Nature*, 455: 1057–60.

Bekhradnia, B., Whitnall, C. and Sastry, T. (2006) *The Academic Experience of Students in English Universities: Summary Report*. Oxford: Higher Education Policy Unit (HEPI), Report 27.

Bell, S. (2007) The dean of arts, *The Australian*, 12 September.

Bender, T. (*a.k.a.* William Pannapacker) (2008) On stupidity, *The Chronicle of Higher Education*, 1 August.

Ben-Shahar, T. (2006) Make lemonade out of lemons, *The Education Guardian*, 25 April.

Ben-Shahar, T. (2007a) *Happier: Finding Pleasure, Meaning and Life's Ultimate Currency*. Maidenhead: McGraw-Hill.

Ben-Shahar, T. (2007b) Cheer up. Here's how, *The Guardian*, 29 December: 36.

Bintliff, E. (2009) French lecturers to hold protests, *Financial Times*, 23 March.

Bone, J. and McNay, I. (eds) (2006) *Higher Education and Human Good*. Bristol: Tockington Press.

Booker, C. (2005) *The Seven Basic Plots: Why We Tell Stories*. New York: Continuum.

Boseley, S. (2009) Drug giant pledges cheap medicine for the world's poor, *Guardian*, 14 February: 1.

Boulton, G. and Lucas, C. (2008) *What are Universities For?* Leuven: League of European Research Universities (LERU).

Bouton, J. (1970) *Ball Four: My Life and Hard Times Throwing the Knuckleball in the Big Leagues*. New York: Dell.

Bowen, W.G. (2008) The successful succession: how to manage the process of picking a president, *Chronicle of Higher Education*, 28 March.

Brabazon, T. (2007) *The University of Google*. Aldershot: Ashgate.

Breakwell, G. and Tytherleigh, M.Y. (2008) *The Characteristics, Roles and Selection of Vice-Chancellors*. London: Leadership Foundation for Higher Education.

Brennan, J., Enders, J., Musselin, C., Teichler, U. and Välimaa, J. (2008) *Higher*

Education Looking Forward: An Agenda for Future Research. Strasbourg: European Science Foundation.

Brothers, C. (2007) Why Dutch women don't get depressed, *International Herald Tribune*, 8 June.

Broughton, P. (2008) *What They Teach You at the Harvard Business School: My Two Years Inside the Cauldron of Capitalism*. London: Viking/Penguin.

Brown, G. (2004) *Britishness*. London: The British Council.

Browning, G. (2008) How to … be content, *Guardian Weekend*, 27 September: 12.

Bunting, M. (2008) Happy mediums, *The Guardian* (Society Section), 30 April: 1–2.

Caulkin, S. (2009a) However good the pay, it doesn't buy results, *The Observer*, 22 February.

Caulkin, S. (2009b) It's time to explode the myth of the shareholder, *The Observer*, 29 March.

Caute, D. (1993) *The Women's Hour*. London: Flamingo.

CHEMS Consulting (CHEMS) (2004) *Final Report to the CUC on Good Practice in Six Areas of the Governance of Higher Education Institutions*, www.shef.ac.uk/cuc/.

Cloud, J. (2007) When Sadness is a Good Thing. *Time*, 27 August.

CMI (Chartered Management Institute) (2008) *Bullying at Work 2008: The Experience of Managers*. London: CMI.

Crews, F. (2007) Talking back to Prozac, *The New York Review of Books*, 6 December: 10–14.

Crook, D. (2006) The Garden House Riot of 1970 and its place in the history of British student protests, *Journal of Educational Administration and History*, 38(1): 19–28.

Crossick, G. (2009) What price excellence? *Times Higher Education*, 19 February: 24.

CUC (Committee of University Chairmen) (2009) *Guide for Members of Higher Education Governing Bodies in the UK: Governance Code of Practice and General Principles*. Bristol: HEFCE.

Cuthbert, R. (ed.) (1996) *Working in Higher Education*. Buckingham: SRHE and Open University Press.

Davies, A. (1991) *Dirty Faxes*. Reading: Minerva.

Davies, L. (2008) *Educating against Extremism*. Stoke-on-Trent: Trentham.

Deem, R. (1998) New managerialism and higher education: the management of performance and cultures in universities in the United Kingdom, *International Studies in Sociology of Education*, 8(1): 47–70.

Deem, R. and Brehony, K. (2005) Management as ideology: the case of 'new managerialism' in higher education, *Oxford Review of Education*, 31: 2.

Delanty, G. (2008) Academic identities and institutional change, in R. Barnett and R. Di Napoli (eds) *Changing Identities in Higher Education: Voicing Perspectives*, pp. 124–33. London: Routledge.

Denning, S. (2005) *The Leader's Guide to Storytelling: Mastering the Art and Discipline of Business Narrative*. San Francisco: Jossey-Bass.

Dillon, H., Smith, A. and Pirou, E. (2007) *Life in the UK Test: Practice Questions*. London: Red Squirrel Publications.

Dugan, E. (2009) Students are revolting: the spirit of '68 is reawakening, *The Independent on Sunday*, 8 February.

Easterbrook, G. (2003) *The Progress Paradox: How Life Gets Better While People Feel Worse.* New York: Random House.

Ecclestone, K. (2007) All in the mind, *Guardian Education*, 27 February: 1–2.

Ecclestone, K. and Hayes, D. (2009) *The Dangerous Rise of Therapeutic Education.* London: Routledge.

Ehrenreich, B. (2007) *Dancing in the Streets: A History of Collective Joy.* Cambridge: Granta.

Elton, L. (2008) Collegiality and complexity: Humboldt's relevance to British universities today, *Higher Education Quarterly*, 62(3): 224–36.

Evans, M. (2004) *Killing Thinking: The Death of the Universities.* London: Continuum.

Farrington, D.J. and Palfreyman, D. (2006) *The Law of Higher Education.* Oxford: Oxford University Press.

Fearn, H. (2008a) Funding focus on research: elite set to split sector, *Times Higher Education*, 27 November: 4.

Fearn, H. (2008b) Sex and the university, *Times Higher Education*, 22 May: 31–5.

Fearn, H. (2009) Faith, hope and the academy, *Times Higher Education*, 26 March: 39–41.

Feynman, R. (2005) *Don't You Have Time To Think?* London: Allen Lane.

Finkelstein, A. (2001) *CAPSA and its Implementation: Report to the Audit Committee and the Board of Scrutiny.* Cambridge: University of Cambridge.

Fisher, S. (1994) *Stress in Academic Life: the Mental Assembly Line.* Buckingham: SRHE and Open University Press.

Fleming, I. (1962) *For Your Eyes Only: Five Secret Occasions in the Life of James Bond.* London: Pan.

Fogg, P. (2008) Academic bullies, *The Chronicle of Higher Education*, 11 September.

Ford, L. (2005) Students' watchdog, *Times Higher Education*, 2 June.

Ford, R. (2006) *The Lay of the Land.* London: Bloomsbury.

Frand, J. (2000) The information age mindset: changes in students and implications for higher education, *Educause Review* 35(5): 14–24.

Frost, R. (1920) The road not taken, in *Mountain Interval.* New York: Henry Holt.

FSSG (Financial Sustainability Strategy Group) (2008) *The Sustainability of Learning and Teaching in English Higher Education: A Report Prepared for the Financial Sustainability Strategy Group by JM Consulting.* Bristol: HEFCE.

Furedi, F. (2004) *Where Have All the Intellectuals Gone?* 2nd edn, including 'a reply to Furedi's critics'. London: Continuum.

Furnham, A. (2004) *Management and Myths: Challenging Business Fads, Fallacies and Fashions.* Basingstoke: Palgrave Macmillan.

Garner, R. (2008) Minister wants to 'lower threshold for complaints' against universities, *The Independent*, 12 September.

Gawande, A. (2007) *Better: A Surgeon's Notes on Performance.* New York: Picador.

Gibbons, M., Limoges, C., Nowotny, H., Schwarzman, S., Scott, P. and Trow,

M. (1994) *The New Production of Knowledge: The Dynamics of Science and Research in Contemporary Societies*. London: Sage.

Goedegebuure, L., Coates, H., van der Lee, J. and Meek, L. (2008) *The Australian Academic Profession: A First Overview*. Mimeo.

Goodyear, D. (2008) I ♥ novels, *The New Yorker*, 22, 29 December: 62–8.

GOS (Government Office for Science) (2008) *Mental Capital and Wellbeing: Making the Most of Ourselves in the 21st Century*. London: Stationery Office.

Gray, P. and Drew, D. (2008) *What They Didn't Teach You in Graduate School: 199 Helpful Hints for Success in Your Academic Career*. Sterling, VA: Stylus.

Guest, D. and Clinton, M. (2007) *Human Resource Management and University Performance*. London: LFHE.

Gup, T. (2008) So much for the information age, *Chronicle of Higher Education*, 11 April.

Guthrie, J. (2008) Down but not out, *RSA Journal*, autumn, 20–5.

Haidt, J. (2006) *The Happiness Hypothesis: Putting Ancient Wisdom to the Test of Modern Science*. New York: Arrow Books.

Hall, A. (2009) *Getting to Grips with Human Resource Management*. London: LFHE/CUC/HEFCE.

Halpern, S. (2008) Are you happy? *New York Review of Books*, 3 April: 24–7.

Hamel, G. (2007) *The Future of Management*. Boston, MA: Harvard Business School Press.

HEFCE (Higher Education Funding Council for England) (2008) *Improving Dispute Resolution: Taking a Fresh Look at Disputes in Higher Education. An Interim Report for Consultation*. Bristol: HEFCE.

HEFCE (Higher Education Funding Council for England) (2009) *Higher Education in England*. Bristol: HEFCE.

Heller, D. and d'Ambrosio, M. (2008) *Generational Shockwaves and the Implications for Higher Education*. Cheltenham: Edward Elgar.

Heller, J. (1979) *Good as Gold*. London: Corgi.

Husain, E. (2007) *The Islamist*. London: Penguin.

i-graduate (2006) HE Career Motivation Study, *Times Higher Education Supplement*, July.

ISI (Intercollegiate Studies Institute) (2008) *New Study Finds Americans, Including Elected Officixals, Earn a Failing Grade When Tested on American History and Economics*. Washington: ISI.

James, O. (2007) *Affluenza: How to be Successful and Stay Sane*. London: Vermillion.

Jeffries, S. (2008) Will this man make you happy?*The Guardian*, 24 June: 12–15.

Kellaway, L. (2009) Management metaphors are truly out for the count, *Financial Times*, 2 March: 16.

Kinman, G. and Jones, F. (2008) *Job-related Efforts, Rewards and Over-commitment: Predicting Strain in Academic Employees*, mimeo, Universities of Bedfordshire and Leeds.

Koole, D. (2008) Glass fully empty, BBC News Online, 7 October.

Koss-Feder, L. (2009) Bunking in With Mum and Dad, *Time*, 2 March: 39–40.

Krugman, P. (2008) What to do, *The New York Review of Books*, 18 December: 8–10.

Lanchester, J. (2009) Is it art? *London Review of Books*, 1 January: 18–20.

Lanning, J., Martin, R. and Villeneuve-Smith, F. (2008) *Employability Skills Examined: Ten Key Messages from LSN's Quest to Understand Employability Skills*. London: LSN.

Lasch, C. (1984) *The Minimal Self: Psychic Survival in Troubled Times*. London: Pan.

Layard, R. (2005) *Happiness: Lessons from a New Science*. London: Penguin.

Layard, R. and Dunn, J. (2009) *A Good Childhood: Searching for Values in a Competitive Age*. London: Penguin.

Leader, D. (2008) A quick fix for the soul, *The Guardian*, 9 September.

Levinson, E. (2007) When keeping your cool counts, *The Times Higher Education Supplement*, 14 September: 14.

Lewis, H. (2007) *Excellence Without a Soul: Does Liberal Education Have a Future?* New York: Public Affairs.

Lewis, M. (2004) *Moneyball: The Art of Winning an Unfair Game*. New York: W.W. Norton.

Lipsett, A. (2008) Study challenges claims of Islamic extremism among students, *The Guardian*, 5 December.

Littell, R. (1993) *The Visiting Professor*. London: Faber & Faber.

Lodge, D. (1988) *Nice Work*. London: Penguin.

Lodge, D. (2008) *Deaf Sentence*. London: Harvill Secker.

MacLeod, D. (2008) What we learned this week. *Education Guardian*, 16 September: 2.

Mamet, D. (1992) *Oleana*. London: Methuen Drama.

Mangan, L. (2008) Five steps to happiness, *The Guardian*, 23 October.

Marmot, M. (2004) *Status Syndrome: How your Social Standing Directly Affects your Health and Life Expectancy*. London: Bloomsbury.

Marr, A. (2007) *A History of Modern Britain*. London: Macmillan.

Mathiason, N. (2009) Can we fix it? No we can't – not during a credit crunch, *The Observer, Business*, 1 February: 4–5.

Mayer, C. (2008) Mean Streets, *Time*, 7 April: 37–42.

McMahon, D. (2006) *The Pursuit of Happiness: A History from the Greeks to the Present*. London: Penguin.

McMullen, J. (2007) The debate about the student contract hots up. WatsonBurton LLP: *Universities Legal Bulletin*, August: 2–3.

McNay, I (2007) Values, principles and integrity: academic and professional standards in UK higher education, *Higher Education Management & Policy*, 19(3): 43–66.

Mickel, A., Dallimore, E.J. and Nelson, C. (2008) What does the pursuit of a high quality of life entail? Grounding a theoretical model in lived experience, *Community, Work & Family*, 11(3): 313–36.

Moreton, C. (2008) The girl with all the brains (interview with Susan Greenfield), *The Independent*, 11 May: 30–1.

Moynagh, M. and Worsley, R. (2009) *Changing Lives, Changing Business: Seven Life Stages in the 21st Century*. London: A & C Black.

NCIHE (National Committee of Inquiry into Higher Education) (1997) *Higher Education in the Learning Society, Report 1: Report on National Consultation*. Norwich: HMSO.

NEF (New Economics Foundation) (2009) *National Accounts of Well-being: Bringing Real Wealth Onto the Balance Sheet.* London: NEF.

OIA (Office of the Independent Adjudicator) (2008) Student complaints on the rise, OIA press release, 14 April.

Osler, A. and Starkey, H. (2005) *Changing Citizenship: Democracy and Inclusion in Education.* Maidenhead: Open University Press.

Oswald, A. (2007) These are good days to be in academia, *Independent Education*, 15 March: 3.

PA Consulting (2008) *Keeping Our Universities Special: Surviving and Thriving in a Turbulent World.* London: PA Consulting.

Park, A. (2009) A primer for pessimists, *Time*, 6 April: 39–40.

Pfeffer, J. and Sutton, R.I. (2006) *Hard Facts, Dangerous Half-Truths and Total Nonsense: Profiting from Evidence-based Management.* Boston, MA: Harvard Business School Press.

Phillips, A. (2008) Happiness studies, *Prospect*, March: 46–9.

Phillips, E., Patterson, D., Bullivant S., Colley, R., Gaster, D., Parsons, G., Pilbrow, G., Punt, S. and Swash, C. (2008) *Mock the Week: Scenes we'd Like to See.* London: Boxtree.

Pilkington, E. (2008) They called me bonkers, *The Guardian*, 27 November.

Pollard, A. (2008) *Growing Old Delightfully,* mimeo.

Prigg, M. (2009) Girls just wanna play iPhones, *Evening Standard*, 6 March: 7.

Ramsden, P. (2003) *Learning to Teach in Higher Education*, 2nd edn. London: RoutledgeFalmer.

Ramsden, P. (2008) *The Future of Higher Education: Teaching and the Student Experience.* York: HEA.

Ross, A. (2008) *The Rest is Noise: Listening to the Twentieth Century.* London: Fourth Estate.

Sastry, T. and Bekhradnia, B. (2007) *The Academic Experience of Students in English Universities: 2007 Report.* Oxford: Higher Education Policy Institute (HEPI).

Schneider, R. and Walmsley, A. (2008) *Dignity at Work and Respecting Difference.* London: Institute of Education.

Schoch, R. (2006) *The Secret of Happiness: Three Thousand Years of Searching for the Good Life.* London: Profile Books.

Schofield, A. (2009) *What is an Effective and High Performing Governing Body in UK Higher Education?* London: Leadership Foundation For Higher Education.

Schuller, T. (2008) A new threshold for learning, *IFLL Bulletin*, 4: 1–2.

Selingo, J. (2008) A midlife crisis hits college campuses, *Chronicle of Higher Education*, 18 July.

Shattock, M. (2006) *Managing Good Governance in Higher Education.* Maidenhead: Open University Press.

Showalter, E. (2005) *Faculty Towers: The Academic Novel and its Discontents.* Oxford: Oxford University Press.

Silver, H. (2003) *Higher Education and Opinion-Making in Twentieth Century England.* London: Frank Cass.

Sims, D. (2005) You bastard: a narrative exploration of the experience of indignation within organisations, *Organization Studies*, 26(11): 1625–40.

Smith, E. (2008) *What Sport Tells Us About Life: Bradman's Average, Zidane's kiss and Other Sporting Lessons.* London: Viking.

Smith, K. (2008) Pelted with cyber-tomatoes, *The Guardian*, 15 July.

Smith, B., Mayer, J. and Fritschler, A. (2008) *Closed Minds? Politics and Ideology in American Universities.* Washington, DC: Brookings Institution Press.

SOMUL (Social and Organisational Mediation of University Learning) (2005) *Working Paper 2.* York: SOMUL.

Spanier, G. (2008) Is campus activism dead – or just misguided? *Chronicle of Higher Education*, 17 October.

Stevens, R. (2004) *University to Uni: The Politics of Higher Education in England Since 1944.* London: Politico's Publishing.

Sutton Trust (2008) *Wasted Talent? Attrition Rates of High-achieving Pupils Between School and University.* London: Sutton Trust.

Tait, S. (2009) PM's plans for 'Britishness' museum consigned to history, *The Independent*, 30 January: 13.

Taylor, D.J. (2007) *Bright Young People: The Rise and Fall of a Generation, 1918–1940.* London: Chatto & Windus.

The Economist (2006–7) Happiness (and how to measure it), December 23–January 5: 33–5.

TLRP (Teaching and Learning Research Programme) (2008) *Education 2.0? Designing the Web for Teaching and Learning.* London: Institute of Education/TLRP.

Townsend, S. (2006) *Queen Camilla.* London: Michael Joseph.

Trow, M. (1989) The Robbins Trap: British attitudes and the limits of expansion, *Higher Education Quarterly*, 43(1): 55–75.

Twale, D.J. and De Luca, B.M. (2008) *Faculty Incivility: The Rise of the Academic Bully Culture and What to Do About It.* San Francisco: Jossey Bass.

UCEA (Universities & Colleges Employers Association) (2008) *A Review of the Implementation of the Framework Agreement for the Modernisation of Pay Structures in Higher Education.* London: UCEA.

UNICEF (United Nations Children's Fund) (2007) *Child Poverty in Perspective: An Overview of Child Well-being in Rich Countries.* Florence: UNICEF Innocenti Research Centre.

UUK (Universities UK) (2008) *Patterns of Higher Education Institutions in the UK: Eighth Report.* London: UUK.

Warner, D. and Palfreyman, D. (2003) *Managing Crisis.* Maidenhead: Open University Press.

Watson, D. (2000) *Managing Strategy.* Buckingham: Open University Press.

Watson, D. (2003) Leadership in UK higher education, in M. Brundrett, N. Burton and R. Smith (eds) *Leadership in Education*, pp. 181–95. London: Sage.

Watson, D. (2005) What I think I know and don't know about widening participation in HE, in C. Duke and G. Layer (eds) *Widening Participation: Which Way Forward for English Higher Education?*, pp. 133–45. Leicester: NIACE.

Watson, D. (2006) *Who Killed What in the Quality Wars?* Cheltenham: QAA.

Watson, D. (2007a) Does higher education need a Hippocratic oath? *Higher Education Quarterly*, 61(3): 362–74.

Watson, D. (2007b) *Managing Civic and Community Engagement*. Maidenhead: Open University Press.

Watson, D. (2007c) Credit where it's due, *Times Higher Education Supplement*, 9 November.

Watson, D. (2008) Universities behaving badly? *Higher Education Review*, 40(3): 3–14.

Watson, D. and Amoah, M. (eds) (2007) *The Dearing Report: Ten Years On*. London: Bedford Way Papers.

Watson, D. and Bowden, R. (2005) *The Turtle and the Fruit Fly: New Labour and UK, 2001–2005*. Brighton: University of Brighton Education Research Centre.

Watson, D. and Maddison, E. (2005) *Managing Institutional Self-Study*. Maidenhead: Open University Press.

Watts, B. (2008) *What Are Today's Social Evils: The Results of a Web Consultation*. York: Joseph Rowntree Foundation.

Weiner, E. (2008) *The Geography of Bliss*. London: Black Swan.

Werdiger, J. (2008) Debt-gorged British start to worry that the party is ending, *The New York Times*, 25 March.

Whitchurch, C. (2008a) Beyond administration and management: changing professional identities in UK higher education, in R. Barnett and R. Di Napoli (eds) *Changing Identities in Higher Education: Voicing Perspectives*, pp. 69–88. London: Routledge.

Whitchurch, C. (2008b) *Professional Managers in UK Higher Education: Preparing for Complex Futures*. London: Leadership Foundation for Higher Education (LFHE).

Whitchurch. C. (2009) Progressing professional careers in UK higher education, *Perspectives: Policy and Practice in UK Higher Education*, 13(1): 2–9.

Wilke, G. (2000) Holding and fragmentation in the organisational mirror, *AUCC Newsletter and Journal*, 1: 2–8.

Wilkinson, R. and Pickett, K. (2009) *The Spirit Level: Why More Equal Societies Always Do Better*. London: Allen Lane.

Williams, G. (2006) Infrastructures of responsibility: the moral tasks of institutions, *Journal of Applied Philosophy*, 23(2): 207–21.

Wilson, E. (2008) *Against Happiness: In Praise of Melancholy*. New York: Farrar, Strauss & Giroux.

Wolin, R. (2001) *Heidegger's Children: Hannah Arendt, Karl Löwith, Hans Jonas, and Herbert Marcuse*. Princeton, NJ: Princeton University Press.

Wyn, J. (2008) *Leadership and Promoting Young People's Wellbeing*, proceedings of the Beijing Normal University and Institute of Education Second International Education Conference – 'Leadership in a Learning Society', Beijing, November.

Younge, G. (2009) Where will we find the perfect Muslim for monocultural Britain? *The Guardian*, 30 March: 27.

Zurlo, J., Rudacille, D. and Goldberg, M. (1996) The three R's: the way forward, *Environmental Health Perspectives*, 104(8).

INDEX

A WILL TO LEARN
Being a Student in an Age of Uncertainty
Ronald Barnett

There is an extraordinary but largely unnoticed phenomenon in higher education: by and large, students persevere and complete their studies. How should we interpret this tendency? Students are living in uncertain times and often experience anxiety, and yet they continue to press forward with their studies. The argument here is that we should understand this propensity on the part of students to persist through *a will to learn*.

This book examines the structure of what it is to have a will to learn. Here, a language of being, becoming, authenticity, dispositions, voice, air, spirit, inspiration and care is drawn on. As such, this book offers an idea of student development that challenges the dominant views of our age, of curricula understood largely in terms of skill or even of knowledge, and pedagogy understood as bringing off pre-specified 'outcomes'. The will to learn, though, can be fragile. This is of crucial importance, for if the will to learn dissolves, the student's commitment may falter. Accordingly, more than encouraging an interest in the student's subject or in the acquiring of skills, the *primary* responsibility of teachers in higher education is to sustain and develop the student's will to learn. This is a radical thesis, for it implies a transformation in how we understand the nature of teaching in higher education.

Contents: *Acknowledgements – Introduction – Part 1: Being and becoming – Where there's a will – Being – Authenticity – Becoming – Part 2: Being a student – Travel broadens the mind – A will to offer – Voice – Dispositions and qualities – Part 3: Being a teacher – The inspiring teacher – A pedagogy for uncertain times – Space and risk – A critical spirit – Coda: Puzzles and possibilities – Notes – Bibliography – Subject index – Name index.*

2007   208pp
978-0-335-22380-0 (Paperback) 978-0-335-22381-7 (Hardback)

LEARNING SPACES
Creating Opportunities for Knowledge Creation in Academic Life

Maggi Savin-Baden

"This is a timely and important book which seeks to reclaim universities as places of learning. It is jargon free and forcefully argued. It should be on every principal and vice-chancellor's list of essential reading."
Jon Nixon, Professor of Educational Studies, University of Sheffield

Learning Spaces sets out to challenge the notion that academic thinking can take place in cramped, busy working spaces, and argues instead for a need to recognise and promote new opportunities for learning spaces to emerge in academic life. The book examines the ideas that:

- Learning spaces are increasingly absent in academic life
- The absence of learning spaces is resulting in increasing dissolution and fragmentation of academic identities
- Learning spaces need to be valued and possibly redefined in order to regain and maintain the intellectual health of academe

This innovative book provides key reading for those interested in the future of universities including educational developers, researchers, managers and policy makers.

Contents: *Acknowledgements – Introduction – Part 1: Re-viewing the landscape – Forms of learning spaces – Creating learning spaces – Part 2: Engaging possibilities – Writing spaces – Dialogic spaces – Reflective spaces – Digital spaces – Troublesome spaces – Part 3: Transforming locations – Boundary spaces – Spatial identities – Repositioning learning spaces – Glossary – References – Index.*

2007   184pp
978-0-335-22230-8 (Paperback) 978-0-335-22231-5 (Hardback)

MANAGING CIVIC AND COMMUNITY ENGAGEMENT
David Watson

"Watson is particularly useful in reminding us about the necessity of strategic thinking (we need to develop 'intelligent' customers and suppliers in the community arena at least as much as for business and industry), about the centrality of values (and the academy's core business of knowledge creation and appraisal), and above all about the role of university staff, students and graduates in helping us to create not only a prosperous economy but also a cohesive community."

Richard Lambert, Director-General, CBI

There is an international revival of interest in issues about the purposes of universities and colleges and their role in a wider society. Much of this is structured around perceptions of the role of higher education in modern knowledge economies. Meanwhile there has been a dearth of scholarly attention to the practice (as opposed to the rhetoric) of civic engagement by universities and colleges in various cultural contexts. This book fills that gap.

It contends that genuine engagement, with the community and with civil society, can be uncertain and risky, but that it plays an essential role in managing today's higher education institutions.

Contents: *Introduction – PART ONE: BACKGROUND – Civic engagement and the founding of modern universities – The UK: the fate of the Dearing compact – University civic engagement in a global context – PART TWO: CASE STUDIES – The UK: the University of Brighton Community–University Partnership Programme – Australia: the University of Queensland Boilerhouse project – The USA: the University of Pennsylvania Center for Community Partnerships – Global benchmarking: the Association of Commonwealth Universities – PART THREE: MANAGING CIVIC AND COMMUNITY ENGAGEMENT – Managing civic engagement: inside the academy – Managing civic engagement: outside the academy – The university community in the community.*

2007   184pp
978-0-335-22046-5 (Paperback) 978-0-335-22047-2 (Hardback)